The Essential Heart of a Leader
12 steps to become the leader that people trust and respect

By
Anthony Munday

Published by New Generation Publishing in 2023

Copyright © Anthony Munday 2023

The author asserts the moral right under the Copyright, Designs and Patents Act 1988 to be identified as the author of this work.

All Rights reserved. No part of this publication may be reproduced, stored in a retrieval system or transmitted, in any form or by any means without the prior consent of the author, nor be otherwise circulated in any form of binding or cover other than that which it is published and without a similar condition being imposed on the subsequent purchaser.

ISBNs:
Paperback   978-1-80369-818-2
Hardback   978-1-80369-819-9
Ebook   978-1-80369-820-5

www.newgeneration-publishing.com

New Generation Publishing

Review of *The ESSENTIAL Heart of a Leader* by Anthony Munday

Unfortunately, we have come to the place in today's work environment where leaders think only of themselves and will base all decisions on the fact that their actions must make them look good in the 'boss's eyes'. The result is a toxic workplace for those who desperately want to do a good job but are buried in red tape and poor leadership. Tony opens the door and allows us to take a peek at the turmoil this practice creates. Then, Tony shows the reader how to be a better leader and how to develop the courage to take on the entrenched system of complacency. Through his real-life experience as a police officer and leader of a police division in Great Britain, Tony uses his expertise and determination to bring about change so that the good men and women who work for him do not have to endure the pain of the traditional "do what I say and don't question anything" leadership they have accepted as the norm. Most importantly, Tony's book encourages the reader to take a hard look at their current leadership role to help the reader come to the understanding that being an exceptional leader means that you "do the right thing – every time – in every circumstance – in every way."

Len Bernat
Author of *Leadership Matters: Advice from a Career USMC Officer*

Contents

The ESSENTIAL Heart of a Leader Prelude 1

Chapter One Your First Day as a Leader Defines You for the Future 7

Chapter Two Bean-Counting Is the Enemy of Leadership 13

Chapter Three The Fatal Illusion of Micromanagement 20

Chapter Four Leadership and Management 27

Chapter Five Setting the Example and Leadership 34

Chapter Six Integrity is the Foundation Stone of Leadership 41

Chapter Seven Honesty in Leadership Is Not Just the Best Policy, It Is the Only Policy 52

Chapter Eight Kindness and Leadership 58

Chapter Nine Courageous Leadership 66

Chapter Ten Leadership is about setting standards that you believe in and others will respect 75

Chapter Eleven Developing Yourself as a Leader 82

Chapter Twelve Leadership Means Knowing Your People 89

APPENDIX ONE 96

APPENDIX TWO 98

Epilogue: my perspective on 'The ESSENTIAL Heart of a Leader 99

The ESSENTIAL Heart of a Leader
Prelude

What have I got to contribute to the myriad of materials on Leadership? Indeed, why should you bother to read any further? The clue is in the title *The **ESSENTIAL** Heart of a Leader*.

This encapsulates my personal experiences and beliefs that leadership is not found by trying to emulate any of the great leaders, like Napoleon or Nelson Mandela. The essential overarching requirement for leadership for me is authenticity. Leadership is about being true to your core values and beliefs.

Ignatius Loyola, the principal founder and first Supreme General of the Society of Jesus (commonly known as Jesuits) said "**Give me the child for the first seven years and I will give you the man.**"

In my case, credit must be given to my parents in this regard. The critical importance of authenticity, being true to yourself and your values and beliefs, was instilled in me by them. Let me share two examples with you.

First, my given name is Anthony. My mum never accepted it being abbreviated to 'Tony'; even in the house, including by my dad.

When I first went to infant school at the age of five, I was placed in a class with Miss STEWART. There was another boy called Antony in the class. She said, "It's too confusing having two Anthony's in the class." Turning to me, she said, "You'll be known as Tony."

I returned from school that day and proudly announced to my mum, "I'm now called Tony," and explained what had happened.

Mum said, "Don't take off your coat, we are going to see your teacher."

We walked the 1.5 miles to school. I was intrigued. We came to the classroom and found Miss STEWART.

Mum said, "Good afternoon, Miss STEWART. My son tells me that you've changed his name for your convenience. My son was christened 'Anthony' and that is how you will address him, please. Are we clear?"

Miss STEWART agreed.

This was an important lesson for me about the authenticity of identity.

During my childhood, my parents developed in me a thirst for knowledge and self-improvement. I was taught by them to read before I was four. I became familiar with books, both fiction and non-fiction. I loved to memorise facts.

Our background was working class. Both my parents worked hard to develop themselves to produce a home that was happy and challenged complacency on any level.

When I was eleven, unbeknown to me, I passed the Eleven Plus which meant I was eligible for Alleyne's Grammar School. The school was founded in 1558; the ethos was akin to a public school. Pupils were drawn primarily from the middle class, professional backgrounds, such as dentists and doctors. It was potentially intimidating.

Mum said, "There will be boys there whose parents earn more than we do. Remember, anyone can be richer than you. No one is better than you."

I should add that my parents supported my brother too. They funded the purchase and development of his business.

These lessons were fundamental in shaping my values and beliefs as a person and then as a leader.

Leadership is all about authenticity.

In the Lower Sixth Form when I was seventeen, as part of our wider education, we students had two weeks of work experience. This was an opportunity to learn about different professions and develop as people. Most others chose solicitors, bankers, and accountants. I chose to spend two weeks with the police department in Stevenage.

It was an eye-opener.

I learned about the demands, challenges, responsibilities, and stress of the job. I also learned that policing has the potential to make a real difference in the lives of the public, both positively and negatively.

The following year, after passing my Advanced Level exams, I was torn between going directly into employment or to university. I remember it was a very hot and sunny day. At the school gates, I met Mr RANSLEY, my Geography and Economics teacher. He was a fearsome character, but he was fair.

I said, "Do you mind if I ask your advice, sir? I have had several offers of employment and offers from several universities. What do you recommend?"

He said, "You can get a job anytime. What you learn at university will equip you for life. My suggestion is that you choose a university far enough from home so that you can learn how to live and take responsibility for yourself." I thanked him and followed his advice.

I studied at the University of Sheffield and had a wonderful time. I got a bedsit and learned (with help from my mum during vacations) how to cook and budget.

I also learned that university was a meritocracy, based on your acumen and intelligence. In academic terms, I learned how to research a topic and produce a reasoned argument in favour of my proposition. This was then subject to challenge from my lecturer and fellow students. If I knew my reasoning was sound, then I would defend it vigorously without regard to popularity.

Making decisions is an important aspect of Leadership. General Colin POWELL makes the following statements about decision-making.

- **"Dig up all the information you can, then go with your instincts."**
- **"Never neglect small details, even to the point of being a pest. Moments of stress, confusion, and fatigue are exactly when mistakes happen."**
- **"And when everyone else's mind is dulled or distracted, the leader must be doubly vigilant. Always check 'small things."**

Some forty years after the conversation with Mr RANSLEY, I discovered that he was Guest of Honour at the annual dinner for former students and teachers. I recalled that he liked red wine, so I bought him a bottle of exceptional claret.

At dinner, I was able to approach him. He remembered me and the conversation! It was highly emotional for me to say, "I followed your advice, sir [I couldn't call him Les]. Thank you for taking the time to listen to me and give me the benefit of your advice." Mr RANSLEY smiled and I was tearful. I was grateful that I had the opportunity to thank him in person.

I later joined Kodak Limited, as a Graduate Accounting Trainee. I spent three years there, becoming part qualified, before I accepted that the generous salary did not compensate me for what mattered to me.

I had joined the Territorial Army to make weekends and holidays more invigorating. They certainly were. I made some great friends there. Over time I took part in several large-scale exercises involving United States

Marines. I learned about the scale and nature of that Corps and the wider opportunities for personal and professional development it afforded.

I visited a Marine Base at Eastcote, North London. I learned a lot more details from one of the captains stationed on the base. He said I'd need a Green Card to be able to be accepted into the officer's training programme. He explained that as a non-US citizen I would not be able to emigrate to join but would need to be employed in the United States. I then decided to create a letter outlining my ultimate intention to join the Marines but explaining to prospective employers that I was willing to provide a sponsoring employer with one year of my services as an accountant.

Over one month, I used the franking machine in the post room at Kodak to send some 300 letters to prospective employers in the US. I received some 100 replies. All but one said that they would be willing to sponsor me, but my honesty precluded them from doing so.

The one who did offer me my dream ticket was a Mrs Mc GREGOR, she owned the World Fishing Company in Delray Beach, Florida. She wrote me a lovely letter. She said that she would sponsor me because I was honest and from England. She said her ancestors came from Scotland. It was not England but was next door. Since I was honest, she would not insist on my working for her at all.

I had not had a holiday for about five years, so I resigned from Kodak. I was enjoying my holiday. Some five weeks later I wrote to her to confirm the details of my arrival. It was bad news. In the interim, her company had been bought out by a conglomerate. They would not honour my deal. I now needed to review my options.

I knew what I did not want, which was repetitive, numerical, and minimal opportunity to use my skills and values for the benefit of others. I kept thinking back to my two weeks with the police as a student. Every incident and activity I had seen and been involved with as an observer was real and meaningful.

My mind was made up. My professional life for the next thirty-four years was about to take shape in ways that I could never have imagined.

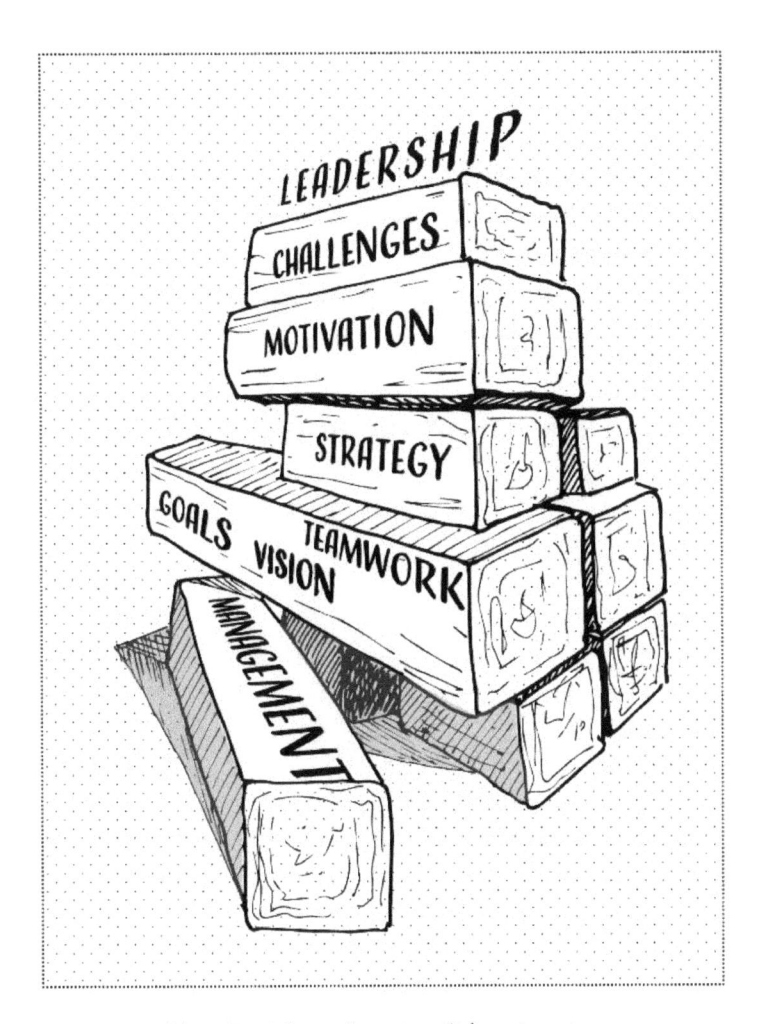

The building blocks of leadership

"Your work is going to fill a large part of your life, and the only way to be truly satisfied is to do what you believe is great work.

"And the only way to do great work is love what you do. "If you haven't found it yet, keep looking and don't settle.

"As with all matters of the heart, you'll know when you find it."

Steve JOBS

Chapter One

Your First Day as a Leader Defines You for the Future

My first day as an Acting Police Sergeant was Thursday, April 14, 1988. It was a blue-sky day. Why has this date remained ingrained in my memory?

I was an experienced officer, with ten years' service at that time. In normal life, it would be fair to say that I was an outgoing, confident individual. That is a keyword: 'individual'. Whilst a team player, my focus was on myself, and my performance, rather than others. Life was about to change for me, in ways I could never have imagined.

I was due to start work at 1400 hours that day. Another person I considered as a friend, Frank MASON, was also scheduled to be on duty, with that team, at 1400 hours. Sadly, whilst walking his dog that morning, Frank intervened in an armed robbery and was murdered.

In those days, news percolated rather than being instant. Cell phone usage was still in its infancy. Eventually, that morning, I became aware of the death of Frank. I remember having to use my landline to phone friends and family to confirm that I was alive. These conversations were awful and bizarre.

At 1300 hours, that day, the 'Management Team' was briefed on what had happened. This included our inspector, me, as the newest member, and the other sergeants. Our principal purpose was to transform many traumatised individuals back into a cohesive, high-performing team.

The lesson of Leadership that I learned that day, was that it was essential for me to know those I had responsibility for as INDIVIDUAL PEOPLE, not just by function. I never forgot this vital lesson that was learned in such horrific circumstances.

The second lesson learned that day was the critical importance of authenticity in Leadership. I was not an automaton or a rank for my grieving colleagues. I was their fulcrum. We were all devastated by this senseless loss of a genuinely nice person. I could not pretend to be empathetic. This was no role play but real life. I had to authentically connect with my colleagues to begin to establish their trust in me as a person who understood their pain and cared about the impact on them as people and professional police officers. They would know if I was faking it. This helped create the trust with those for whom I had responsibility and became the cement that bound the team together.

In my view, these two lessons enabled me to understand that Leadership is about accountability and responsibility towards those you have responsibility for. Leadership is not self-centred. It is externally focused on creating an environment that energises the team and develops people to their maximum extent.

The lessons in Leadership that I learned that day stood me in good stead for the next twenty-four years of my police career. At every occasion that I inherited responsibility for new teams or departments, my priority was to authentically connect with them as people before developing performance management and strategy.

Before that day, I had believed that Leadership was about being the 'shining star' in every aspect of operational activity. In other words, I would have to pretend to be the best at every single aspect of policing. An impossibility as well as being far removed from reality.

Marshall Goldsmith said, **"What got you here, won't get you there."** Wise words indeed.

Leadership was less about 'me' than about 'us'. I learned that Leadership is a sacred privilege, not a rank or title. Understanding that I had responsibility for the welfare, wellbeing, safety, and aspirations of other people is humbling but not demoralising. But remember. Although leadership is primarily externally focused, we must not neglect ourselves. 'Burn out' can occur if we do not ensure our own resilience.

It is said that 'animals smell fear'. In the same way, I believe that people 'smell a fake'. What do I mean by that? Simply put, the Leader's words, behaviours, and actions are not aligned. This creates fear, distrust, even contempt amongst others in the team.

Why does this happen? There are several reasons – including insecurity and a lack of belief in their ability to fulfil the requirements of the role of Leader.

In my direct experience, the worst 'Leaders' shared common behaviours. They did their best to avoid challenging or difficult decisions. They were quick to blame others for not having the benefit of 'hindsight' when the situation was fluid. They focused on self, so they engaged as 'evidence gatherers' for their next promotion or assignment – falsely claiming credit for the work of others. They were micromanagers with a desire for perfection of outcomes that were unrealistic. They became known as 'Olympic Torches' (they never went out) because they rarely left the police station to go to the scene of the action. As a result, these Faux-Leaders were invisible to those for whom they had responsibility. The team was unknown to them as PEOPLE. They did not care.

The corrosive impact of these negative behaviours and mindset on the team was a breakdown in trust and transparency with the Faux-Leader. Quality of performance, morale, sickness all suffered.

It does not have to be like this. Authenticity, allied with an appropriate mindset and behaviours, transforms the experience of being a Leader. Leadership with its associated responsibilities becomes a refreshing responsibility rather than an onerous series of tasks. The result was that I could perform at my very best as a Leader because I remained true to my values as a person.

The benefits to the organisation were quickly evident. This type of Leadership would produce a high quality of performance delivered by a team that embraced decision-making and challenges because they were supported by their Leader. This was realistic and made possible because we knew each other as PEOPLE.

When you know that those for whom you are responsible are choosing to deliver their highest quality of performance for the benefit of the collective team then you have reached the sweet spot. This is not complacency. It is a recognition that people are doing their best under the current circumstances. The context will change and develop, as does the team.

"Setting Goals is the first step in turning the invisible into the visible."

Tony ROBBINS

Bean counting is the enemy of leadership

Albert Einstein is attributed to have said, "Not everything that can be counted, counts. Not everything that counts can be counted."

Chapter Two

Bean-Counting Is the Enemy of Leadership

All organisations should adopt not just the words that define their 'Higher Purpose' but the culture that empowers and refreshes it. The higher purpose is the Mission Statement expressed in emotionally intelligent terms, such as how clients and team members feel as a result.

Target Culture is injurious and at times fatal to the True Purpose of the organisation. The True Purpose for employees is not the pay packet but the spiritual wellbeing that results from working there.

Customers value the quality of their organisation and how you make them **FEEL** after their experience of interaction with you. The drone-like processes that impact upon customers to regard them as numbers or 'tick in the box' are cancerous to all concerned.

In my experience, the 'bean-counters' success in 'proving' their increased business efficiencies is often pre-ordained because of sponsorship and support at the Executive Level.

The essence of policing in the United Kingdom is with the consent of the public. The foundation of modern policing is found in the Principles of Law Enforcement by Sir Robert Peel established in 1829 (see Appendix 1). Sir Robert Peel was the Home Secretary who introduced the Metropolitan Police Act of 1829. He subsequently became a Commissioner of the Metropolitan Police. A very rare example of a politician having to do what he had required of others! These Principles clearly outline the Higher Purpose of Policing.

These Principles for Policing were unique at the time.

They underpin the ethos of an essentially unarmed police service in the UK, which is rare in the world today (see Appendix 2).

Since 2010 in the United Kingdom, there have been significant cuts to police budgets and officer numbers have fallen some 21,500 out of a total of 144,000. A further 7,000 Police Community Support Officers (PCSO) were lost. This has resulted in police strength at its lowest level since 1981.

The response of chief constables has been to 'suck it up'. They have sought to stem the shortfall by selling their capital assets, such as police stations, to fund current expenditure. That is potentially disastrous.

An alternative strategy would have been for these self-styled 'Leaders of the Service' to challenge the rationale of the cuts in terms of public confidence and feeling of safety. Instead, 'efficiencies' were sought in terms of reducing the number of police stations, significantly worsening the terms and conditions of officers. This led to an increase in the rates of retirement, resignations (particularly of experienced officers), and reducing the accessibility of police to the public.

In operational terms, officers were brigaded into fewer stations. Business processes including investigation of crimes and non-confrontational contact with the public deteriorated rapidly. Also, this new operational strategy added to the concerns of climate change by increasing the carbon footprint of the organisation since officers had to travel much longer distances and the associated timelines for this travel were increased.

The 'bean-counters' insisted that having fewer stations from which officers patrolled would enable support services to be delivered more effectively as they were based in those fewer stations. The significantly negative operational impacts described above were ignored. To adapt a phrase, bean-counters know the cost of everything and the value of nothing. They are inwardly focused on the costs, structure, systems, and processes of the organisation, without sufficiently valuing the higher purpose.

The True Purpose for which I joined the police was not the pay, as I had accepted a near 50% reduction in salary compared to being a trainee accountant. I joined to 'make a difference' in the lives of everyone I met. As a result, I can share with you the lessons learned.

Leadership is doing the right things for the right reasons at the right time.

In my direct experience, the most toxic form of Leadership is when those in positions of responsibility and authority impose numerical- based targets on organisations. They have the mistaken belief that their approach is business-like and is an authentic and accurate measurement of operational delivery. The reality is quite different.

The phrase 'what gets measured gets done' summarises neatly the impact of this form of Management on the culture of the organisation. Like a waterfall, this 'accountability' flows downwards, which is the antithesis of Leadership.

This form of Leadership is essentially lazy. It enables people who are paid to take responsibility to absolve themselves of this and become bookkeepers who tick boxes. This is instructive as to their mindset and behaviours. They deliver their feedback remotely – usually by the ubiquitous email or by an underling.

These behaviours destroy any pretence of credibility by these managers. Invariably they exhibit fear and alarm at the implications of the decision-making for fear that it would hurt their smooth and uninterrupted progression up the corporate ladder. Perhaps most significantly these negative behaviours are felt by their teams or departments.

Leadership is knowing ourselves and those we are responsible for as people and behaving accordingly.

This is an alien concept to such people. Often, they feel uncomfortable having 'difficult conversations' with people, even on the most basic level, such as 'How are you?' let alone 'What do you think about...?'

Leadership imbues the organisation in the 'Higher Purpose' that is critically important to deliver sustained success and that demands significant, sometimes extreme (as in military operations) levels of voluntary commitment by the team.

The damage caused by this simplification of the true purpose of the organisation is that motivation is damaged for those for whom they are responsible. There is no 'Big Picture' or Business Strategy to energise and engage people. It is a dumbing down of perspective.

Another negative aspect of the 'bean-counting' mentality is the corollary of 'Gaming'. This is when actions and behaviours are skewed to such an extent that they have a corrosive effect upon the 'Higher Purpose' of the organisation by those who deliver operationally. People realise that they will be evaluated, praised, or criticised based on the attainment of the 'Targets' which often have little or no bearing on what matters to the customers, the general public.

At its worst, lives are lost or unnecessarily damaged and the brand reputation of the organisation is tarnished – sometimes irretrievably.

Throughout much of my police service, I was on the receiving end of a style of 'Management' that can be encapsulated in the phrase 'What gets measured gets done'. Quantity-based targets are far easier to 'measure' than qualitative ones. Government-directed 'Performance Targets' concern the most simplistic approach to policing, indeed, the wider 'Blue Light' Community. The following examples will suffice:

The time taken for an operations room call handler to pick up the phone, despatch a unit to the situation and for that unit to arrive is measured. Almost identical 'performance indicators' are used for the Ambulance and Paramedic Service. What is missing is an appreciation of the context and the quality of the outcome.

When I became an inspector, the reality of this culture hit home. I was 'held to account' concerning the numbers of activities that my teams and departments delivered. My strategy was to look at this issue from the 'supply' rather than the 'demand' side. My responsibility as a Leader was to equip those for whom I was responsible with the requisite skills and confidence to maximise their **quality of performance**.

To achieve this, I had 'heavy lifting' to do. This was to **know those I had responsibility for as individuals**. This provided an accurate barometer of capabilities and potential. The time invested in doing so enabled me to ascertain authentically and accurately who was inexperienced, who was a toxically poor performer, who was incompetent, who was competent, and who was outstanding. The result was that it was now possible to plan and develop the capabilities of my team or department with confidence and trust. The result was that our teams and departments delivered to their maximum and gave of their best in every situation. Invariably, the 'numbers' were positive too!

Bean-counting provides a superficial take on the performance of an organisation. I truly believe that an organisation stands or falls by its people and their active engagement in taking personal responsibility for delivering the strategic purpose. In policing, this can be saving lives, thus promoting the safety of the public and maintaining the Queen's Peace.

The personal impact on me, as a person and as a leader, was that I regained significant portions of time for me to use to best effect, for the organisation, team/department, and myself.

To be clear, quantity-based 'performance indicators' are exactly that. Leadership has a responsibility to deliver a quality of performance that is appropriate and realistic. The true measure of performance is the reaction and engagement of customers with that organisation.

"Don't count the days, make the days count."

																			Mohammed ALI.

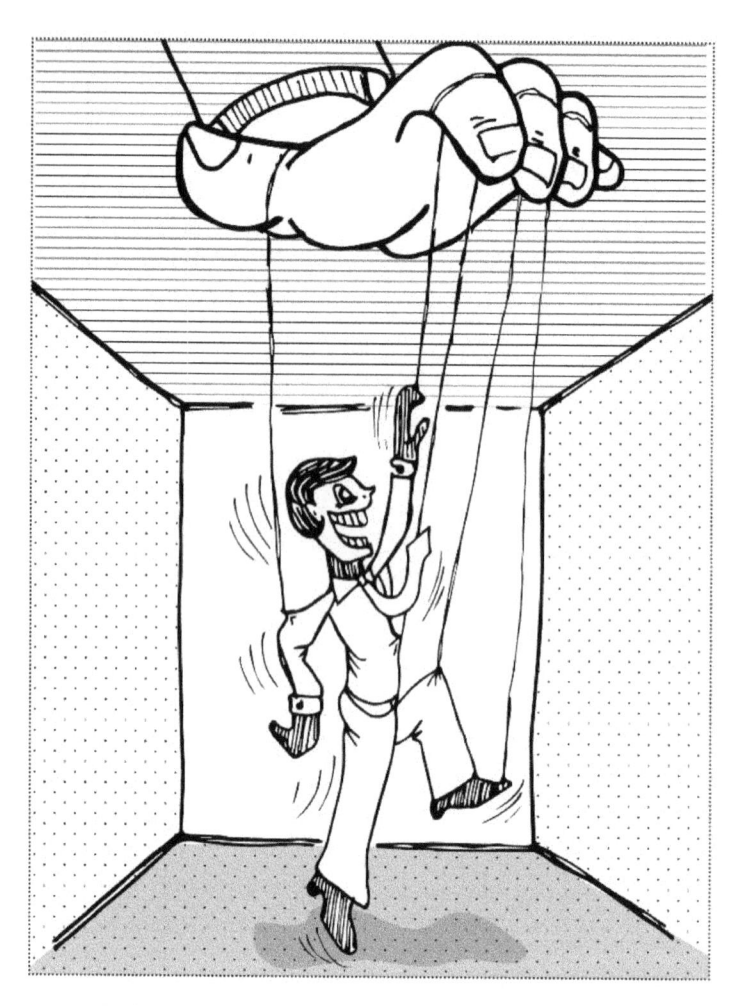

"The Department of Micro-management"

"It doesn't make sense to hire smart people and tell them what to do. "We hire smart people, and they tell us what to do."

Steve JOBS

Chapter Three

The Fatal Illusion of Micromanagement

At its heart, micromanagement is based on several flawed premises.

At its most basic, if I, as a manager, stood beside an individual making and receiving calls all day, or working, using a laptop, I would not necessarily know the context or history of their communication with the person on the other end of the line. I would not necessarily even know the position and responsibilities of that other person nor the purpose of the call, or the reason for the search history on the laptop.

If I were to watch a person communicate digitally, similar blind spots would exist.

My experience as a senior leader in the police is that micromanagement essentially reflects a lack of trust on the part of a manager with those for whom they have responsibility.

Trust is the cement that binds the team together, enabling it to perform at its peak level and quality of performance. It is the responsibility of the Leader to earn the trust and respect of their reports. The positive traits that help this to occur include visibility, credibility, consistency, and fairness.

A lack of trust on the part of the team with their Leader reflects several factors. Negative traits, which undermine trust, include selfishness, duplicity, absence at times of significant stress on the team, and a lack of
emotional intelligence.

I saw it as a prerequisite that, whenever I took responsibility for a new team or department, I made it a priority to get to know my colleagues as people and vice versa. We all understood and adhered to the chain of command, but I never needed to refer to my rank to make things happen. We had a commonality of interest.

I knew people's family circumstances, birthdays, favourite football teams, outside interests, personalities, and ambitions for the future. They knew mine. It enabled us to perform to our best for people we knew. The result was my team never felt like anonymous numbers in a unit. Leadership is knowing ourselves and those we are responsible for as people and behaving accordingly.

I had the misfortune to discover the A, B, C, D style of Leadership at several stages of my police career. The mnemonic stood for '**A**ccept nothing, **B**elieve Nobody, **C**heck everything and **D**ocument it'. As you can see, this methodology was founded upon a complete lack of trust amongst those colleagues who, in a literal sense, should have 'had your back'.

I also had the misfortune to be on the receiving end of this version of Leadership. Did I feel valued, respected, motivated by these behaviours? Of course not!

The shocking point is that this 'Leadership Style' became endemic on many occasions. In an environment where simplistic, quantity-based 'performance targets' were the norm (e.g., numbers of outcomes per officer, such as arrests), the 'zeal' with which senior 'managers' imposed this 'Target Culture' sometimes tipped over into bullying behaviours.

An illustration of how a seemingly innocuous 'Target' can distort activity and corrode respect for the 'chain of command' can be found thus:

'ALL officers must arrest "x" persons per month.' If I may, I will concentrate on the true performance implications of this instruction.

Firearms officers were 'held to account' over this target. It was not unknown for them to 'volunteer' to arrest shoplifters! Similarly, roads policing officers, whose visibility, expertise, and educational role is highly significant, were also subject to this instruction. In both cases, their highly valuable, valued training and expertise did not necessarily bear a close correlation with numbers of arrests. This, distortion of Leadership was highly damaging for individuals, the organisation, and the public at large.

The more senior colleagues who practised 'ABCD' Leadership did not indicate respect for those over whom they had responsibility. Those on the receiving end of these behaviours were more concerned with 'covering their backs' than the credibility and value of the mission. On a personal level, these 'ABCD' people would have found their role to be a lonely one. What would it be like to behave in this fashion?

Leadership is a privilege and should be focused upon the principles of 'kaizen' or 'Continuous Improvement' of the organisation. It is all our responsibility to drive a business forward, not just the CEO.

In my view, authentic Leadership is founded upon mutual trust and respect between all levels of the team. It is not a 'free pass' to be indolent.

I inherited responsibility for a team that was regarded as a byword for poor performance and errant behaviours. I knew the departments where the data was collated. I explained that I was taking responsibility for the
team. I was told "good luck with that!"

I asked who the poor performers on that team were; that is, experienced people whose behaviours were toxic at best, cancerous at worst. The same names were provided: three sergeants and six constables.

My team consisted of ten sergeants and sixty constables. This poorly performing team had been 'indulgently micromanaged' by my predecessor. The culture consisted of much 'upwards decision-making'. Officers referred decisions to a higher level of authority to such an extent that my predecessor was ensnared in tactical decision-making, rather than strategic Leadership. The result was a stream of emails and reports which were not backed up with appropriate action.

I needed to deliver my message in person to my new colleagues. The logistics of their deployment meant that it took a month to personally deliver my messages.

In policing in the United Kingdom, the day starts with 'Morning Prayers'. This is the term used to describe what is supposed to be a strategic review of the preceding twenty-four hours of policing activities. Instead, it is often a 'shooting party' where decisions are micro-analysed, second-guessed, and victims for criticism found by those who rarely venture out into the murky world of operational policing. **The result is a defensive, 'cover your back' mentality and behaviours by operational officers.**

I needed to break this log jam that came from 'top-down' decision-making to create a team that was able to think for itself. So, my initial interaction with my team to outline the new 'norm' that was initiated by me was designed to enable them to perform as trained with the understanding that I was willing to stand up for them. Indeed, I confirmed that it was my responsibility to do so.

I began my remarks, "I need you to make decisions. Record the rationale for your actions (e.g., saving a life) and the relevant information available to you at the time. This will help with formal proceedings later, such as criminal courts.

"I will support you. If there is criticism from senior colleagues, then that is my responsibility, and I will be held accountable. If there are lessons to be learned, so be it. We will use that lesson so that we all learn."

The veracity of my pledge took time to become embedded. Trust began to develop and grow, and we began to work as a team. The result was that after six months, we had moved from fifth place to third in the 'performance table'. After one year of being led instead of being micromanaged, we were the top-performing team.

Interestingly, at no time did I refer to the numerical performance 'targets' against which we were measured. My colleagues performed to their maximum. The numbers looked after themselves.

I enjoyed the experience of being a Leader. Knowing that the individual team members were delivering their best quality of work, because they understood why it mattered.

Leadership is accountability and responsibility.

"A boss who micromanages is like a coach who wants to get in the game.
"Leaders guide and support and then sit back to cheer from the side lines."

Simon SINEK

"I hope this is all CLEAR?"

"Management is doing things right; Leadership is doing the right things."

Peter DRUCKER

Chapter Four

Leadership and Management

It is more complex than that. Management for me signifies order and structure. Leadership is disruptive in business terms as it is continually challenging the status quo to deliver better outcomes.

Organisational culture evolves to become more relevant or it is becalmed and sterile where standards are maintained but the environment rarely changes.

For example, in the police departments in the United Kingdom, there existed height restrictions that differed according to your gender. These were later abolished under Equality legislation as leaders began to understand that physical strength plays a part in the capability of an officer, but it is not the most important attribute. Emotional intelligence and good communication skills are absolute requirements and are unrelated to stature.

Leadership contains elements of management but is not constrained by it. These include organisational structure and line responsibilities.

Management is task-focused, whilst Leadership is about exploring opportunities to develop systems and people. Management is often tactical by nature, whereas Leadership is more strategic.

In my career in the police, I was often regarded by more senior colleagues as a maverick. I was regarded as a person who had to believe in the strategic purpose and operational impact of decisions, rather than ignoring them, and blithely acting as a cipher for someone else's decisions.

'What gets measured, gets done.'

On too many occasions during my career with the police, 'Performance Management' was a term used freely, and invariably referred to **Poor** Performance. This focus was unfortunate on many levels. It also distracted managers into an unhealthy obsession with poor performers. This had the downside of ignoring two categories of people: competent and outstanding – the very people you want to encourage and help grow in their duties and responsibilities!

The cultural impact of these behaviours and practices of managers was that they were not stretched to perform. Quantitative-based targets did not challenge these two groups to excel. What they did was either 'good enough' for the manager or they challenged and motivated themselves. Both cases are, in my book, a failure of Leadership.

A 'tick-box' mentality is often associated with poor managers. Their mindset, behaviours, and values are transmitted to their teams. 'Anything for a quiet life' means that the team realises what will satisfy their 'manager' and that becomes the norm.

Key Performance Indicators are just that. They do not define the totality of a performance or, necessarily, the qualitative aspects, which relate to **how** this is delivered and the true **impact** of delivery.

The most sophisticated systems of 'Performance Management' can and are defeated by the values exemplified by the 'manager'. I have personal experience with this.

In my previous organisation, 'appraisals' were replaced by 'Performance Development Reviews' (PDRs). The change was introduced by email. There was no meaningful engagement with staff at the operational level, (constables, sergeants, and inspectors) as to the rationale or cultural significance of the change. The emphasis was on the 'clarity' and 'efficiency' of this online platform.

The credibility and value of the system lay in the honesty and commitment of the appraiser to the appraisee. The process was heavily 'top-down'. The words and definitions of the behavioural competencies were fine. The delivery left a lot to be desired.

A Key Performance Indicator (KPI) was 'getting the PDRs done' within prescribed timelines, rather than the quality of the content and engagement of staff. A colleague proudly told me that he inserted the words 'on track' for each behavioural competency and graded everyone as 'competent'. This sorry excuse for a manager was never challenged by his team or his line managers over several years. The result was that this person's toxic behaviours and attitudes meant authentic performance management did not exist for him nor his subordinates.

How do you begin to quantify the true cost to the organisation, the people, and this person of this endemic derogation of Leadership when this nonsense was 'signed off' by more senior line managers and extended up to the executive level?

My behaviours were somewhat different. I recognised that the platform was a more efficient way to collate and evidence performance; that the value of PDRs was intrinsically bound up with how it was presented to my colleagues and subsequently used.

Therefore, I explained to my people that it was a significant responsibility of Leadership to develop people to the maximum quality of performance and provide relevant, timely evidence of confirmation. I ensured that all my teams and departments understood the processes and their value.

The impact is nicely illustrated by the example of a team that had not had the benefit of a meaningful PDR for three years before I inherited responsibility for them. Previously, the PDR was regarded as a 'task' rather than an opportunity to motivate and recognise fairly the standard of performance for an individual over the year.

The team was comprised of non-police officers, known as police staff. According to their terms and conditions, when police staff delivered outstanding performance this should be recognised by increment payments, which were consolidated into their pensionable pay.

The Chief Constable had described the performance of the team as 'outstanding' in a Major Incident that occurred three years previously. This had been recognised by a Departmental Commendation. This was the catalyst for a change in culture that I was seeking; and intending to introduce and embed.

I asked the team, individually, and then as a group, as to how they could evidence their quality of performance if they wished to be considered for internal or external jobs under the current 'system'?

The 'penny dropped' and the point was made. They gathered their evidence of performance for the previous three years using corporate systems and submitted their PDRs to me.

I quality-assured the work and spoke to the HR Business Partner for our business unit. Reluctantly, she accepted the logic and fairness of the evidence. Their pay was appropriately adjusted and backdated accordingly. The team was amazed and grateful and I had won their trust to believe in me. I explained that my predecessors and the organisation had failed them.

My responsibility to them, as a Leader, was to recognise in a fair and timely manner the standard of performance and ensure that their aspirations for development were appropriately met.

I have coined the term 'Performance Leadership'. This means that we have a duty of care to pay due regard to the development of all those for whom we are responsible. Those who are often ignored or forgotten, the competent, to make them better; and the 'good', to make them outstanding. These groups deserved to have their performance recognised in a fair and timely manner. This includes developing people out of your team.

Poor performers deserve appropriate support and guidance, but not tolerance. Otherwise, as Leaders, we fail everyone for whom we have responsibility.

"Management is about persuading people to do things they do not want to do, while Leadership is about inspiring people to do things, they thought they never could."

Steve JOBS

Strategic Thinking

"Set high standards for yourself and don't settle for anything less. "You are the best judge of yourself and your capability."

Tony ROBBINS

Chapter Five

Setting the Example and Leadership

It is common to talk of 'hard skills' and 'soft skills' when discussing Leadership and Management.

'Hard Skills' is a term used to describe our technical and sector-specific competencies. In my case, as a police officer, this included how to use Corporate IT systems, the knowledge of criminal law, and understanding how to implement proper police procedures. That is what we do.

'Soft Skills' is often a pejorative term implying it's the 'soft and fluffy' aspects that covers everything else. Essentially, the people elements. That is how to motivate others to follow when we are in a leadership position.

Unless we are exercising our authority in an appropriately strict command and control manner (as when dealing with life-or-death decisions), obtaining authentic buy-in for our proposals is the key to authentic and successful Leadership.

In my case, the realisation that, as a Leader in the police department, my responsibilities were not focused on my arresting people or dealing with them for Road Traffic Act offences as it was early in my career.

Unfortunately, my Leadership role began during the height of the 'Target Culture', where the leaders stressed that what gets measured gets done. The unintended result I witnessed was seeing firearms officers at the end of the month (when figures are collated) volunteering to attend stores to arrest shoplifters to achieve their 'target of arrests.' As ridiculous as this practice was, very few of my senior colleagues challenged this nonsense.

In the proper execution of their duties, it would be an authentic performance indicator for firearms officers to arrest armed criminals or to prevent such offences by intelligence-gathering and pre-emptive arrests before more substantive offences are committed.

It was essential for me as a Leader and as part of my professional development to recognise operational absurdity when I experienced it and to effectively and appropriately challenge it. I felt confident in my responsibility to do so because of my confidence in understanding the nature of Leadership.

Leadership creates the values, environment, and culture of the organisation. It enables those for whom we are responsible to deliver their best quality of performance and to empower them with the understanding that their contributions are vital to operational effectiveness.

I had and still have a voracious appetite for continuous self-improvement and development. I call this Personal Kaizen, after the Japanese culture of the same name which relates to organisations. The essence of this mindset, is the question 'can we do this better?' I will give the following example, to illustrate my mindset.

When I joined the police in 1978 as a constable, it was a common viewpoint amongst my supervisors and experienced colleagues that, as part of my professional development, it was a good experience for me to be able to complete a crime file. This consisted of all the attendant paperwork required at court for a person I had arrested.

The most common offences for my 'debut' were thefts from retail premises, which was called Shoplifting (contrary to Section 1, Theft Act 1968); and a person Drunk and Incapable, that is, drunk in any highway or other public place or any licensed premises (such a public house) contrary to the Licensing Act 1872, Section 12. I had discovered the existing culture, of 'this is what we do here.'

Several years later, I was a sergeant performing custody officer duty at Watford Central Police Station. The operational area was the busiest in my organisation. My principal responsibilities were to ensure the legality of arrest of persons and process their detention expeditiously and safely.

The day was a Thursday, and my tour of duty was 1400 – 2200 hours. This was known as 'late turn' and was invariably busy. I was responsible for the safety and wellbeing of a maximum of eleven detainees.

That day, there were six detainees on 'constant observation'. This meant that their physical condition was so compromised by the amount of alcohol they had consumed that six police officers were required to constantly monitor them, rouse them regularly, note their condition, and make the appropriate report. The result – there were fewer officers available to respond to calls for service from the public in our area!

That evening, we had a visit from the police authority (governance body). I explained the impact these detainees were having on our operational capability. They were essentially medical emergencies rather than criminals. Their repeated behaviours meant a 'revolving door' into police detention. We were wasting our time, rather than dealing with the core issues. I won the support of the police authority to investigate the wider strategic issues.

I presented a business case to a senior colleague, outlining an alternative way of dealing with such detainees in a problem-solving way. I included a case study of the opportunity cost of police arresting and detaining an individual, demonstrating that in one year, the cost was £96,000. This did not include the costs of court procedures. My senior colleague supported my work.

I developed a good professional relationship with the Forensic Medical Examiner (FME) who examined the fitness of detainees for detention. We created a Working Party, comprised of representatives of the local NHS Hospital Trust, the Ambulance and Paramedic Service, local borough council, and a local charity. The charity worked with persistent drunk people to uncover the cause of their addiction and to help them recover from their addiction by having a variety of professionals to provide the necessary counselling and assistance. As important as this step was to help those with the addiction, this long-term solution to the problem made it possible for the addict to relapse and, once again, be arrested.

I researched the topic and discovered that the offence of Drunk and Incapable had been de–criminalised in Scotland for many years. The Working Party recognised that we were dealing with medical emergencies and social issues rather than a criminal offence. We developed a protocol seeking to lawfully divert drunk and incapable persons from custody.

My senior police colleague, the chairman of the charity and I presented the protocol to the Permanent Secretary at the Home Office (the most senior civil servant in that department, who advises the Home Secretary), since this Minister of the Crown had the ultimate responsibility for the Criminal Justice System.

This Home Secretary has the ultimate responsibility for the governance of the Criminal Justice System in England and Wales. The Home Secretary subsequently enacted the legislation to make our protocol the first example of persons lawfully diverted from custody in England and Wales.

Police officers and professional colleagues began to recognise such persons as medical emergencies rather than potential performance targets. In time, my work was codified as Doctrine (National Best Practice) by the National Police Improvement Agency (NPIA) and my actions set the example for my team that tackling problems is not just the right thing to do – it is your responsibility.

I played a full part in developing a training programme, with my working party colleagues. It was invigorating and challenging to work in partnership, creating a holistic response that was both practical and lawful.

The programme was delivered to all operational police officers, plus colleagues from other services. Initially across our borough, and subsequently across the organisation.

Most importantly, it helped instil an understanding amongst my colleagues, that by reframing our thinking, we saved a huge amount of time, effort, and energy, as well as helping to change people's lives for the better.

The feedback that we received was very powerful.

I remember an individual, a senior manager, who had personal problems.

He had sought escape from his issues by going to Watford, to become habitually insensible with intoxicating liquor. He was seriously contemplating suicide.

He was found by police officers and lawfully diverted to the authorised, alternative Place of Safety, rather than the police station.

The expert, patient, and supportive care that he received helped him to turn his life around.

I received a letter from his daughter, thanking me for helping to save the life of her dad.

"Rank does not confer power. It imposes responsibility."

Peter DRUCKER

"I have your back NO MATTER WHAT"

"A true leader has the courage to stand alone, the courage to make tough decisions, and the compassion to listen to the needs of others.
"He does not set out to be a leader but becomes one by the equality of his actions and the integrity of his intent."

General Douglas MACARTHUR.

Chapter Six

Integrity is the Foundation Stone of Leadership

Integrity creates the trust that cements the Team together.

Integrity is defined by the Cambridge English Dictionary as:
"The quality of being honest and having strong moral principles."

We cannot always foresee when our character will be put to the test. In my case it occurred, quite unexpectedly, one New Year's Day. I was a constable of three years' service, at this point.

I had been extremely busy during the preceding days and had amassed a significant workload, which was time sensitive.

Bank Holiday working attracted double time payment. It was most unusual to be required by my sergeants to complete my pile of paperwork during the eight hours of that shift, rather than be deployed operationally.

I did not have my issue truncheon with me as I was 'forbidden' to leave my desk by my sergeants.

I was beavering away completing paperwork.

I had my police personal radio tuned to the local police channel when I heard the excited voice of a colleague, Dave M shout "10-1. Officer requires urgent assistance!" He gave a location, and then there was an ominous silence.

The code 10-1 was sacrosanct. It meant an officer was in a very perilous situation. All officers who heard that call were duty-bound to strain every sinew to attend as swiftly and safely as possible.

I immediately left the office I was in and almost collided with the duty inspector.

"Have you got a car?" he said.

I replied, "No, sir."

"Jump in with me then."

We arrived at the location, just in time to see Officer Dave M being headbutted by a known offender. (The officer's nose was later found to be broken.)

I exited the car and approached the offender.

He was 6 feet 2 inches tall, and a champion boxer. He was exhibiting all the indications of being aggressively intoxicated. He came towards me, swearing and having his fists clenched.

I instinctively punched him on the chin, with all the force I could muster, and he fell to the floor.

Just as I did so, I heard the screech of brakes and a criminal associate ran towards me and the Inspector.

We grappled with his associate and fell through a hedge of a nearby garden.

The offender was very powerful, swearing and threatening to kill us both.

I looked up at the front window of the house, and saw a lady drinking a cup of tea. She looked startled.

The inspector was known for his dry sense of humour.

He said, "Lad, I don't expect you thought you'd be rolling in a garden, being punched, before nine o'clock on New Year's Day?"

I had to agree.

Other officers arrived, and both offenders were arrested.

The inspector saw my bruised knuckles and torn, bloodstained uniform. He instructed that I be examined by the duty police doctor at the police station. The purpose was to confirm the nature and cause of my injuries.

Older, more experienced officers at the police station saw me before I was examined by the doctor.

Both offenders had made official complaints of assault against me, to the custody officer.

"What are you going to say about your injuries to your hand?" they said.

I replied, "That I punched them both because they were violent, and it was a reasonable response on my part."

"You'll be in trouble at court, and they've made complaints. You should say you fell over and grazed your knuckles."

"It's the truth, and that is what I'm telling the doctor. It will also go into my witness statement."

"You must be mad."

Due to the seriousness of the offences, the case was heard at a Crown Court several months later.

Whilst waiting for my turn to give evidence, the prosecution barrister came to the witness room.

He introduced himself and said, "Have you seen the pictures?"

I looked confused.

He produced an exhibits album and I opened it to be greeted by a set of full-colour photographs of the incident.

They had been taken by the householder whose garden I'd been in with the inspector.

The first picture showed my right fist connecting directly on the chin of the offender who had headbutted my colleague.

The barrister said, "I must commend you, Officer. Not just for your actions on the day, but for telling the truth to the police doctor, and in your witness statement.

"If you hadn't done so, you'd now be in extremely serious trouble. I personally know a number of officers who have come to grief in similar circumstances by rewriting the reality of incidents."

Both offenders pleaded guilty and received custodial sentences.

There is a postscript to this case study.

Several years later, I was in a pub, off duty with a police colleague.

I was in the male bathroom, washing my hands, when I was confronted by the second offender (I had been with in the garden) from that incident. He was known to be an extremely violent man.

I tensed, he then smiled, held out his hand and said, "I was out of order.

You did what you had to do. Fair play to you. Are we all square?"

We were shaking hands when my police colleague burst through the door.

He had clearly been expecting the worst.

I swiftly explained.

The takeaway for me throughout my police career, was 'a lie is always a lie.'

Leadership for me, is founded on the principles and morality imbued in me by my parents, and schooling.

Simply put, if I was ashamed of my values and behaviours, then I am letting myself down, and those for whom I'm responsible.

In my direct experience, leadership in the police departments in the United Kingdom can be described as 'Command and Control'. That is: "Do as I say, I'm a higher rank than you", "Do this because this is what we do", and sometimes "Do this because I'm ordering you to." I am not referring to Situational Leadership, but the style and culture exhibited as a matter of course by too many.

I was fortunate to be accredited in coaching as a leadership style. This had a profound effect on me. My subsequent behaviours as a leader were regarded as 'maverick' by peers and colleagues. I took that as a badge of honour because I referred to the people in my teams and departments as "Those for whom I have responsibility" rather than "Those I command".

Throughout my service, at different stages, I was exposed to the spectrum of leadership, from the outrageously poor to the inspirationally excellent. In retrospect, the key features that determined my assessment of Managers and Leaders were:

- Could I believe in that person to do the right thing for the right reason?
- How trustworthy were they?
- What was their track record of evidenced behaviours?
- Was it important for them to take time and trouble to get to know me as a person?
- Were they willing to demonstrate appropriate support to complete the mission?
- Did they micromanage or did they help their team grow as individuals?
- Did they trust in me to determine the tactics to achieve the strategy?
- Did they demonstrate honesty?
- When making assignments or administering corrective action, did they demonstrate fairness?

In other words, I was able to consistently perform at my best because a colleague 'had my back'. Three words that mean so much. In the same way, colleagues I trusted knew that 'I had their back'. Integrity means being honest and having strong moral principles.

Relations between police and young people are often problematic and confrontational. These tensions and stresses may be exacerbated by issues of race.

The disproportionality of representation and outcomes with Black and Minority Ethnic (BAME) people in the Criminal Justice System in the United Kingdom is a fact. The reasons and causes are argued over.

A process called Stop and Account was being proposed by the Home Office to reduce confrontational issues between the police and public. I was the project manager for my police organisation for this work. I organised a Project Team consisting of representatives of all stakeholders within the police who were involved in its development and delivery. I decided that total transparency of process was required to gain the trust and confidence of all stakeholders in the development, and delivery of the project.

I also ensured that two members of the Independent Advisory Group (IAG), (community representatives who monitored and scrutinised police activity) were full members of that Project Team.

My methodology was also to share proposed changes with those who would be impacted by the new procedures with the User Group. These included operational colleagues who represented different units. I decided that the required Person Specification for the User Group was to have a positive mindset but sceptical. The intention was to 'test to destruction' the proposed changes.

Feedback received would be honestly assessed and, where necessary, amendments would be made to the policy. The project was successfully delivered on time and within budget. I conducted a Post Project Review to learn the lessons and disseminate them accordingly.

Shortly afterward, a new Chief Constable was appointed. He made it clear to other executive-level colleagues that he considered this work bureaucratic nonsense. The support for the implementation amongst senior colleagues withered away. This was disappointing and cowardly.

A senior colleague and I were invited to meet with the Chief Constable and Deputy Chief Constable (DCC). The DCC had been the Executive Lead for the Project and had been an enthusiastic supporter. Throughout the meeting, the DCC remained silent whilst the Chief Constable rubbished the Project.

At one point the Chief Constable said, "We are only doing this work because a few dark people complain."

I replied, "With the greatest respect, Chief Constable, you are wrong," and explained why. The silence was deafening.

The following day, I was present at a meeting of senior leaders and the Police Authority (governance body) for the presentation of the New Year's Policing Plan. The venue chosen was The Grove Hotel. This was an extremely plush venue. It was intended to signify the significance of the event. The Chief Constable delivered the presentation by PowerPoint.

When a slide entitled 'Diversity' appeared, he said "Diversity is the golden thread that runs throughout policing. It's never about the legal minimum." Such breath-taking hypocrisy from the Chief Constable lessened my respect for his leadership.

Coincidentally, at the next two promotion boards, my evidence was adjudged insufficient by one mark each time, thus preventing me from proceeding to the final interview part of the process.

It was an awful feeling to realise that this was the reality of my position.

I was never going to be successful at any promotion panel whilst this Chief Constable held sway over my professional life.

I did not sulk or slink away into the night.

I considered the option of transferring my services to another police organisation, but I knew that would be futile. There are many ways in which my candidature could and would be undermined by my Chief Constable.

I concentrated on becoming the best person and best Leader that I could be. I refused to countenance compromising my Ethics and Values.

Leadership is doing the right things for the right reasons at the right time. Honesty means eradicating wilfully poor performance once there are no reasonable causes for it, such as lack of knowledge, experience, or resources. This is fair for all concerned.

Leaders have responsibility for people as well as resources. Our people trust us to regard their wellbeing and resilience seriously. However, risks cannot be removed from all operational decisions.

We are trusted to evaluate those risks and explain the rationale for our decisions where appropriate. Trust is the cement that binds the Leader and the team together.

In my direct experience over several decades, it could easily be regarded as the ESSENTIAL trait of leadership. The calibre of relationships and communication determines the quality and effectiveness of operational delivery and performance.

At its most critical point, when I was required to place those for whom I had responsibility in harm's way, I needed them to trust in my decision-making and leadership. This was paramount to the successful outcomes we achieved together. I never lost sight of the fact, that I was dealing with the lives and wellbeing of those for whom I had responsibility, including colleagues, 'customers' (victims, witnesses, suspects) and the public.

Throughout my career, both in the private sector and in law enforcement, I was very much aware that leadership is a privilege, not a job title or rank. I believe that knowing colleagues as REAL PEOPLE helps imbue leaders with recognition and respect for what will be required of all of us to 'complete the mission'. This means being familiar with names, family details, birthdays, interests, aspirations – that is the reality behind the mask.

My credo is:

Leadership is knowing ourselves and those that we have responsibility for as people and behaving accordingly.

The 'big picture' or strategic intent of our actions must be borne in mind, but a leader must never forget that every life is precious, none more so than the other.

All lives matter.

Trust enables Leadership to engage, energise and empower the full potential of our colleagues. Such additional 'discretionary effort' imbues all of us to achieve more than we thought possible.

To adapt Thomas Edison's quote, **"Leadership is 99% perspiration, and 1% inspiration."**

Trust amongst the team is based on evidenced behaviours and actions taken by leaders. These will be sufficiently strong to overcome personal agenda issues or hearsay from others. We spend so much time at work it can only be beneficial to enhance that experience through human contact.

Trust in leadership is a two-way street. Leadership is not delivered by email but by 'walking the walk'. Leaders have a duty and responsibility to themselves and to others to ask appropriate questions of those senior to us who require us to implement a strategic purpose.

Phrases such as 'Pin your ears back'; 'This is an instruction, not a request'; 'Do as I say'; 'This is how we do things here' are insufficient in themselves to absolve a leader from responsibility. 'The Nuremberg Defence' i.e. 'I was merely obeying orders' had a limited shelf life.

Simply put, if we, as Leaders, do not believe in what we are about to impart to those for whom we have responsibility then how can we expect those colleagues to believe and comply?

Authentic Trust creates a symbiotic relationship between the leader and the team. When it exists, it creates an aura and intensity that is palpable and real. It is a good place to be.

There is a feeling of 'higher, common purpose' that helps us to give of our best more often and more powerfully. It helps create a common identity or culture that is embracing but not suffocating. In business terms, performance is enhanced and consistent.

Leadership, for me, is far more about 'we' and 'us' rather than 'me'. Leadership has soul. Demonstrated Integrity in the leader imbues the team with a warm glow of confidence in the quality of the decision-making process of the leader. This enhances operational efficiencies and promotes a positive culture in the team with a 'can-do' mindset.

"Integrity is the most valuable and respected quality of leadership. "Always keep your word."

Brian TRACY

"The business is growing everyday!"

"Honesty is the fastest way to prevent a mistake from turning into a failure."

James ALTUCHER

Chapter Seven

Honesty in Leadership Is Not Just the Best Policy, It Is the Only Policy

Honesty is the fulcrum of effective Leadership. Honesty starts with us accepting our limitations and the nature of Leadership.

Leadership is not about being a 'Superstar' – the best performer at every task or activity within our teams. Rather, it is our responsibility to create the environment and culture whereby others choose to perform to their maximum quality of performance for the benefit of the team.

Honesty is about saying what we mean and meaning what we say. Honesty is about being appropriately humble whilst being determined to develop a culture of good behaviours, teamwork, and focus on delivering the mission.

It is a terminal failure of Leadership to be known or caught out by others being duplicitous, economical with the truth, or, heaven forbid, lying.

In my direct experience, when there was a realistic prospect of operational needs resulting in serious harm to my team, I never 'sugar-coated' the message. Leadership required me to ensure that the relevant Risk Assessment Process had been conducted realistically and truthfully. For example, if the Field Marshalls in the First World War had been required, or chose themselves, to experience the horrors of trench warfare and the suicidal futility of 'going over the top' for a small advance, paid for in oceans of blood, then their devotion to the 'Big Push' might have produced a radical change in thinking.

I knew my teams as people. I realised that their trust in me was based upon my operational experience and our awareness of each other as people. When you look at each other in the eye rather than sending an email or getting a subordinate to deliver your instructions, then communication is at its most real and intense. We were a team, not a random collection of individuals. It would be unforgivable if I did not share the potential dangers with them by my visibility and presence.

Honesty in Leadership includes setting standards and ensuring adherence. It is not about hectoring or bullying the team. It is the quiet confidence that you can feel in well-led teams that know and understand why these standards matter.

Honesty includes ruthlessly eradicating wilfully poor behaviours and standards. It is a question of fairness to everyone in the team. It is the responsibility of Leadership to ensure that these standards are inculcated in less experienced colleagues correctly. When we ask our team to go above and beyond, there must be no doubt of its purpose and rationale and that all team members can perform in a manner that protects the team.

Values and mindset are the foundations of Leadership behaviours. Honesty is the key to create an environment and culture of mutual trust and respect. The knowledge that those for whom we have responsibility rely upon us as Leaders to keep them safe is a grave responsibility.

In my police career, there were circumstances where members of the team were in harm's way because of decisions that were taken by me. Dynamic Risk Assessments provide a methodology to mitigate Risk but cannot eradicate it. This Dynamic Risk Assessment was accomplished by ensuring the pre-planned operations followed the IIMARCH Structure (Information, Intention, Method, Administration, **Risk,** Communications, Human Rights, and other legal issues) to mitigate the risk and ensure each team member was aware of the risk they would face during the operation. Being completely honest during these operations saved lives.

Honesty pervades Leadership decisions and behaviours across the board. It is not merely inconsistent to exhibit honesty in some respects but not others, it is highly corrosive to the trust that ensures team cohesion. The ability to harness honesty should be considered a significant strength. Honesty not just in terms of relating to subject or matter but in self-honesty – how ethical and integral behaviour is mirrored.

Honesty in all our interactions with each other is vitally important. Whenever I had to impart information or decisions, I was conscious of the need to deliver the message clearly and unequivocally truthfully. Any failure on my part to do so was disrespectful to the person(s) concerned and the wider audience that would hear about it.

Reputation is like a first impression on meeting someone. Once you have soiled your reputation, it can never be rebuilt. Remember, reputation is what people say about you when you are not there.

Similarly, for myself, whenever I had the misfortune to meet a duplicitous colleague, I discounted them as an authentic colleague once I had realised their value set. They became 'virtual persons' who were disengaged from the operational reality. They were not to be trusted.

In the instances of duplicitous colleagues who were more senior to me, they were regarded with withering contempt. They were 'virtual Leaders' who existed in their own delusional 'bubble'. Colleagues can always smell insincerity. It may appear on the surface as a form of perfection, neatly set out or packaged, but once that bubble bursts what oozes out is dishonesty. Dishonesty not only stinks but it is highly infectious.

It is rare in policing for Leaders to rely on their rank to affect actions. My direct experience was that where they did, these persons were, indeed, 'virtual Leaders'. Invariably, they were sad people who had, by their duplicity, excluded themselves from that which is best about organisations – authentic human interactions and honest feedback. The consequences of a lack of honesty in Leaders can be felt across organisations and amongst the people.

Glossy Mission Statements on the organisation/company website or premises which loudly proclaim (that) 'People are our greatest asset', when Leadership is dishonest, run a significant risk of facilitating the development of a toxic culture.

People do not like to be taken for granted or treated like fools. In the end, dishonesty fools no one. Colleagues may not inevitably like honesty, but they will trust and respect it. When there is a task to be undertaken, an order to follow, an action to pursue, respect and trust trumps whether the action is popular or not.

Conversely, honest Leadership, which lives and breathes the Values indicated in that Mission Statement, reinforces a positive, performance-minded culture.

Dishonest Leadership in an organisation or company results in poor performance, disengaged teams and people, a lowering of morale, increased sickness rates, stress, and absenteeism.

Good people will read the signs and act accordingly. They will leave your business, thus impacting negatively upon your Brand and the quality of your customer service. It becomes a downward spiral from which recovery is virtually impossible because they will go elsewhere and although you may never encounter them again, the stories they relate about your business practices will impact upon your wider reputation forever.

The business costs of stress induced by poor Leadership behaviours are considerable. In the United Kingdom in 2017, statistics from the Health and Safety Executive indicate the following:

- **Cost of Staff Turnover, £2.4 billion.**
- **Cost of sickness absence, £8.4 billion.**
- **Cost of reduced productivity at work, £15.1 billion.**

What are the costs to your organisation or company?

"Leadership can be defined in one word, honesty.
"You must be honest with the players and honest with yourself."

Earl WEAVER

TEAM

Together
Everyone
Achieves
More

Better Together

Chapter Eight

Kindness and Leadership

General Colin Powell shared these insights on the significance of kindness in delivering effective Leadership:

- **Being kind doesn't mean being soft or a wuss.**
- **Kindness is not a sign of weakness. It is a sign of confidence.**
- **If you have developed a reputation for kindness and consideration, then even the most unpleasant decisions will go down easier because everyone will understand why you are doing what you are doing. They will realise that your decision must be necessary and is not arbitrary or without empathy.**
- **As the old saying puts it, "To the world you may be one person, but to one person you may be the world."**

In my view, kindness in Leadership is being respectful and fair to those people who have entrusted their professional lives to me. This is a significant responsibility because, being in the profession of law enforcement, there would be occasions when they will be put in harm's way.

When I inherited responsibility for a new team, my top priority was for us to understand and know each other as people. The reason for this is because there are circumstances in which I will have to command them – to issue an instruction that for reasons of safety or lifesaving, I needed them to follow my command without question. By taking the time to understand each other as people, a bond of mutual respect formed, thus achieving total trust in the correctness of my decision-making process. This enables the team to deliver effective operational cohesion and achieve our intended objectives.

It is most important to appreciate that not all decisions or actions will have life-threatening consequences but the unexpected can happen. In those situations, there is often little or no time to ponder alternative strategies to resolve the issue. This is when the trust built during non-stressful situations becomes the foundation for trusting in the rationale of the leader's quick directions and decisions.

Knowing each other as people is not about being intrusive. It is about knowing each other sufficiently well so that my team understands that their wellbeing is as important to me as my own. In my case, this includes family, birthdays, sports, interests, and passions.

I am a Chelsea Football Club fan. I say this because sports are an area where we can share common likes or dislikes, totally removed from the structure of our working environment. The balance of sharing time with work colleagues off duty is a delicate one. Leadership recognises the potential pitfalls of crossing the line. The behaviours in watching a match together in convivial social settings are not analogous to operational reality. But in many ways, I found that because we spent social time together, a sense of team bonding developed rather than anarchy. We had all been trusted to know each other as people. This was respected.

On the rare occasions that there was an 'overspill' from the social setting to the workplace, I ensured that the faux pas was swiftly dealt with in a professional, measured manner. Invariably, the team member would be apologetic rather than resentful. We all make mistakes. The issue is not to repeat those mistakes, so they become habit forming. This would jeopardise the cohesion of the team and the positive culture that we had built up.

In many respects, Leadership comes from the heart.

Leadership has soul.

That is, it has a spiritual quality. It is founded upon a keen interest and understanding of the people for whom we are responsible – their welfare, wellbeing, performance, and development. Our teams are not made up of robots but people with a range of feelings, desires, interests, hopes, fears, and passions. In other words, our team members reflect you.

It is the privilege of Leadership that people entrust their present and futures to us. This is a leasehold situation with terms and conditions, both formal and informal, rather than a permanent acquisition.

I described kindness as fairness. I meant by this that expecting high-performing colleagues, who demonstrate a positive morale, to subsidise the wilfully poor quality of performance from lazy or workshy colleagues, is unfair.

The first order of business in taking responsibility for your team is to evaluate them critically and objectively in terms of the requirement of their roles and responsibilities. A Training Needs Analysis process will help inform future development of your team in terms of capability and capacity.

Wilfully poor performers are toxic for your team's culture, your peace of mind, and your reputation. In my experience, such people are akin to errant children. They know the reality of their behaviours but do not seem to care, whilst the professionals among your team are watching the leaders to see if these poor performers will be held to account.

Whenever I inherited responsibility for a new team, I would arrange individual meetings with colleagues, starting with the poor performers. I would ask them for their view of their performance. Invariably, it was glowing and rosy. I would evidence why this was a false picture of reality. I would ascertain if I were dealing with a 'would not' or 'could not' situation and deal accordingly.

Where there were development issues in terms of professional competence, then support and mentoring to achieve the required standards within a designated timeframe was provided.

The others were a form of 'internal saboteurs' and were more insidious to the health of the team culture. Those who felt that professional standards were an optional extra in their case were advised that their continuance as part of the team was not an option for them. They had decided to chance their fate to luck and it had run out. Available options for them were transfer to an alternative location, without a positive reference from me, or a change of career.

In my view it would not be kind to them or other members of the team to permit them to continue to undermine the culture and quality of performance required. I was not prepared for myself or my supervisors to spend time micromanaging them – waiting for them to commit a career-ending infraction that would be 'too hot' for them to handle. The opportunity cost in terms of support for their colleagues plus that of the morale of myself and my supervisors was a price I was not prepared to pay.

Similarly, I would inherit teams who had been 'indulgently micromanaged' by a previous inspector – where the leader relies extensively on emails and written reports to convey strategic direction and develop the culture of their teams. In such circumstances, these faux leaders were often regarded as 'good people' by the poor performers and held in contempt by those who strove to be the best that they can be. This is not kindness; it is failing to perform. Another characteristic of such people is that their indolence and neglect of their responsibilities created a paralysis of decision-making. There was a vacuum of decision-making at the point of delivery of service.

It is not a kindness for leaders to fail to imbue members of the team with the ability and confidence to make decisions when required. By not delegating this responsibility to your team member, you will stifle morale, reduce operational effectiveness, and keep quality peers from growing in their leadership capabilities. This scenario is akin to those people who copy others into emails as though this absolves them of responsibility.

Kindness, delivered with respect, is a powerful emotion and enabler.

Because of cost-of-living issues associated with working in Hertfordshire, many police officers in my organisation, lived a good distance away from their workplace and area of operations. Car ownership was a necessity rather than a luxury. Since policing is a twenty-four-hour service, officers are required to work shifts to ensure an effective delivery of service. The servicing of our cars is based on a combination of the usage, condition of our cars, and the availability of time slots at the garage. Sometimes, the team member's car was booked in for a time that may make that colleague late for duty. I asked team members to always speak with me about the circumstances of the appointment. I evaluated their rationale and, when appropriate, permitted team members to keep that appointment and attend for duty as soon as possible. This was kindness, not softness.

I knew the calibre of the person I was dealing with and trusted their veracity. They knew they were being trusted and that their colleagues were sharing a heavier workload because of their temporary absence. I never had a situation where this trust was abused. I also rationalised that a poor performer would not have had the confidence to inform me of their predicament. They would have taken leave of absence through 'sickness.'

For kindness to be credible in a leader, there must be empathy amongst the team. The most extreme situation in the police, in which I demonstrated kindness to colleagues, was in the aftermath of the murder of a popular team member shortly before he was due to attend work. We were all traumatised by this senseless tragedy. Our colleague had been walking his dog when he came upon an armed robbery in progress and was shot dead.

Most of my colleagues were alone with their thoughts. Some were crying. My responsibility was not to think of my own pain but to assuage their individual and collective grief to the extent possible. My objective was to provide those words and behaviours that could start the healing process for them and to enable them to begin to reconfigure themselves as a cohesive team. In conjunction with other professional support, we achieved our objective.

Leadership is knowing ourselves and those for whom we are responsible as people and behaving accordingly.

"We rise by lifting others."

Robert INGERSOLL

Courageous Leadership

"Be humble. Have the courage to speak the truth."

Ken POIROT

Chapter Nine

Courageous Leadership

Courage comes in many forms. It is about doing the right thing, particularly where there are implications for the wellbeing or safety of the leader. The risks of action or inaction need to be objectively assessed but sometimes, this can be a 'gut feeling'. Instinct is based upon subconscious experience as to what is the right thing to do for the greater good of the team or organisation – never oneself.

I like the above quote because having the courage to do the right thing is based on values and ethics rather than point-scoring or self-promotion.

Organisational culture can be described as 'the way we do things here.' Ideally, the culture should be positive, appropriately respectful of people, and empowering.

Sometimes, leadership can be a lonely furrow. We choose to say or do the right thing because it is the right thing to do. It is courageous leadership to challenge the status quo when the consequences of your inaction or acquiescence negatively impact appropriately and professionally upon the wellbeing or lives of others, including oneself.

I was the Project Manager with the responsibility to deliver significant cultural and operational change for my police organisation. We were one of five pilot sites of what would develop into a national change programme, sponsored by the Home Office.

Policing activity towards Black and Minority Ethnic (BAME) communities, particularly, younger people, was subject to significant concern and challenge. I learned a new word – 'disproportionality'. This term referred to the differences in outcomes for young BAME people compared with that of the white population. This was a highly contentious topic for me and other colleagues to accept and digest. In discussions, none of us accepted that we were prejudiced.

Government data indicated that in BAME encounters with the police, the outcomes were more severe in terms of sanctions than with the white population. The severity of outcomes extended across the Criminal Justice System; from initial contact, arrest, judicial disposal (charge), bail or incarceration awaiting trial, and finally, the nature and extent of sentencing. In several respects, we were in a state of denial.

As Project Manager, I was given time and support to research these issues thoroughly. This meant that I was better able to appreciate the views of BAME communities than would have otherwise been the case.

I recall a video that had been developed jointly between the young people of Lambeth, a deprived, diverse Borough in London, and the Metropolitan Police Service (MPS). The video showed young people and operational officers discussing their interactions. The video was raw and honest – capturing the challenges of policing young people.

As part of my research, I visited a Community Association for people of Afro-Caribbean descent. The audience consisted of adults. The picture they painted of police interactions with their young people was extremely depressing. It was essentially confrontational with little positive communication with their local police. The language used startled me. It was akin to describing an occupying army.

Because I felt the issues were generic, the video was shown in every police team training event across the police organisation. The hope being that this video would demonstrate the absolute need for change.

I attended a training session in that same town less than a week after I had visited the Community Association. When the video was shown to the officers, they were outraged and dismissive of its relevance to them. Once I explained the feedback received from the parents and grandparents of the BAME young people in their town, they were stunned. I discussed the positives of the video. It showed the unvarnished viewpoints of police and young people that had a history of distrust between the groups. This was the perceived reality and provided the opportunity for both groups to understand the other's viewpoint.

It was important to develop a culture within my police organisation that would authentically embrace the need for change and deliver a better quality of service for our communities. Part of my strategy for the Project Team was for every operational department to be represented by a sceptical and positive person. I did not need or desire to have imposed upon me those people who were merely negative and distrustful of change. I ensured this happened by attending meetings of the Command Teams (senior officers and police staff) of every strategic department in the organisation, such as Crime Management.

In the first instance, I listened to their concerns about cost, bureaucracy, relevance, and impact upon operational policing. I answered their questions honestly and fully. I explained that the change was going to happen. It was a real opportunity to develop policing links with young people positively. The change, when properly implemented and embraced by the departments, would benefit the police and the public. Once agreement had been reached, I requested that a member of the relevant Command Team introduce each and every training event and to express their positive support for the change programme. This was unprecedented. I explained that for this change programme to become embedded, the senior leaders needed to confirm their support to their officers and staff.

Another relevant example is the change I helped facilitate was the way police dealt with High-Risk Missing Persons. Young people, up to age eighteen, who were in the care of the Local Authority were placed in accommodations where a social worker had management and pastoral responsibility for them. Invariably, these young people had a range of problems including behavioural and educational issues. Their reluctance to conform to the rules and regulations of these establishments meant that once they had breached them and left the building, the social worker reported them as missing persons to the local police.

The incidence of young people going missing during the hours of darkness and returning in the morning was very high. These young people were regarded as a nuisance rather than vulnerable. So lax was the mutual concern for their wellbeing that a proforma was developed which was faxed to the local police station for purely administrative purposes. There was no initial investigation until after 0800 hours when the daytime social worker would confirm their return or otherwise. If the young person had returned, there was a cursory interview by the social worker and the case was closed. These circumstances were regarded by senior police officers as an efficient way to deal with inconvenient tasks.

I challenged this thinking and explained my reasoning to a senior colleague. These young people were described as children under criminal law. They were highly vulnerable and should be regarded as High-Risk Missing Persons. I obtained approval to evidence my concerns and to devise a new system.

At that time, there were two twenty-four-hour operational police stations in the two boroughs which formed our Police Area. I knew the capabilities of the Station Duty Officers (SDO). These were non-police officers who had an inquiring mind and were familiar with police systems of working. The SDO conducted initial risk assessments and inquiries on the proformas. Where they ascertained reasonable lines of inquiry, they informed the Duty Inspector who allocated an appropriate person to investigate. If the missing person was of serious risk to their health or wellbeing, a detective officer was allocated to deal with the situation. When the young person was found, they were interviewed by appropriately trained officers.

As a result of my work, I created a Missing Persons Unit staffed originally by the two SDOs. The proforma was abolished and the appropriate documentation was used. Dealing with vulnerable young persons had been regarded by many senior officers as a time-wasting exercise in futility. I transformed that mindset into an intelligence-led approach to risk assessment and the investigation and protection of vulnerable young people. Our work prevented many vulnerable young people from coming to greater harm.

Leadership is doing the right things for the right reasons, at the right time.

The processes concerning the reception and management of persons detained by the police is one of the most critical business functions of police organisations.

Many of the legal aspects are contained within the provisions and Codes of Practice of the Police and Criminal Evidence Act 1984, commonly known as PACE.

This is because the welfare, wellbeing, indeed lives of prisoners has significant ramifications for the individuals concerned, police officers dealing with them, police organisations, the wider Criminal Justice System, and Society.

Despite these truths, the role of Custody Officer (a police sergeant with direct personal responsibility to ensure PACE is complied with and the detainee's welfare needs are met) is not necessarily regarded in an appropriately positive light by their respective Senior Officers.

Sergeants performing the role can regard it as a poisoned chalice for themselves, in terms of the severe implications of 'things going wrong' during their tour of duty. The role and responsibilities of Custody Officer can easily lend itself to significant stresses and micromanagement. In many ways the custody officer is an extreme version of reactive Servant Leadership.

Custody Officers can see themselves as often in a 'no-win' scenario as the gatekeepers between the detainee and police officers investigating the offences for which they have been arrested. These feelings and behaviours can impact negatively on feelings of self-worth.

The cultural stereotyping by police organisations of undervaluing the role of Custody Officers can result in the importance of their personal and professional qualities being downplayed.

In my police organisation, each Borough had its own Custody Suite.

There was a lack of performance management and quality of service amongst the Custody Suites across the organisation.

These issues were recognised at Executive level in the organisation.

A Criminal Justice Department was set up to devise and develop a more cohesive strategy.

My role, with my colleague Mark, was to create and lead the detailed work of implementing the change management processes necessary to move from ten Custody Suites line-managed locally, to four sites, line-managed and led centrally.

Change can be disruptive for people, as well as invigorating.

Most importantly, we had to develop a coherent team, with the consistent Values and Behaviours that would provide an improved quality of service to our stakeholders, and a better culture and environment for the emerging team.

Mark and I had never worked together before or known each other.

It was an invigorating experience for me to develop my Leadership skills in a partnership context. We developed a positive and cooperative system to objectively assess all aspects of Custody Suites, including inputs and feedbacks from those at the operational side who invariably have vital business intelligence to impart.

Before introducing changes, we met with stakeholders to establish 'their reality'. We listened, asked questions, and became better informed as to the priorities for change, that would provide most benefit to the team and the organisation.

One of the most significant aspects of change was to facilitate a less confrontational attitude between different units that increased both business efficiencies and improved the culture for the team.

We then devised a training programme for the team, that recognised their responsibilities, and introduced a fair and objective performance management system.

We did not pretend we knew all the answers. However, by our visible Leadership that developed trust and credibility amongst the team, we began to build a consensus for change.

Custody had been treated by some as a sinecure for 'too difficult to handle' staff.

We established whether we were dealing with a 'can't do' or 'won't do' situation, and developed people, or offboarded them accordingly.

Leadership cannot be delivered by email.

It was essential for us and the team to know each other as people and behave accordingly.

Positively intentioned ideas were welcomed from the team. We evaluated, trialled, and implemented them as appropriate.

As a direct result of input from meeting members of the team face to face, we established a team newsletter that provided valuable business intelligence as well as 'personal notices' such as professional development, social events and matters of interest, e.g., birthdays.

This was an extremely popular and useful method of helping to develop a team identity and a positive, engaged culture.

Mark and I developed a strong bond of commitment and trust with the team that was evident.

We developed agreed quality standards in service delivery with the team and for ourselves.

Formerly, Custody could be regarded as a grim and foreboding place to be, where officers making discretionary arrests would first check to see which Custody Officer was on duty before making that arrest!

The culture was changed to a cooperative, inclusive environment, where self-induced stressors were minimised, for the benefit of those working within the Custody Suite.

In an appropriate sense, people smiled more, and sought positive, practical solutions to issues, rather than erect unnecessary barriers to an investigative colleague.

It was a wonderful way to sign off from my police career.

"Courageous leadership is not fearless leadership. "What makes you a leader is how you deal with your fears."

Andy HARGREAVES

Understanding the bigger picture

"A genuine leader is not a searcher for consensus but a moulder of consensus."

Martin Luther KING Jr.

Chapter Ten

Leadership is about setting standards that you believe in and others will respect

In my direct experience, leadership comes from the heart, not the head. To remind a leader of this important fact, the leader needs to be able to look at themselves in the mirror each day and believe in the person staring back at them.

Any of us, at any time, can pretend to others, by words or behaviours, to be anything we choose to be. Actors do this all the time. The best of them research their subjects thoroughly and immerse themselves to the extent possible. They will gather information on how particular types of people behave. In the cases of playing famous people, they will adapt their posture, wear similar clothes, have the same hairstyles according to photographs or newsreels of such people. They will adopt mannerisms and hire a voice coach to sound as near identical to the celebrity as is humanly possible. They will repeat famous speeches word perfectly for the camera.

There are people in many walks of life who have rank or titles, wear an impressive uniform, but they are acting the role of the leader. They have programmed themselves to have the trappings of position but not the inner belief that they understand the nature and responsibilities of leadership. Such faux leaders are invariably self-centred, focused on their next career move, and evading liability for decisions that could 'come back to bite them'.

In my personal experience as a police officer, I was subject to the Criminal Law and Police Regulations which defined the lawful behaviour I was to exhibit each day in the performance of my duties. The 'why' included saving life, arresting offenders, and protecting the vulnerable. The 'how' I operated as a leader was founded upon my values and ethics that had been inculcated in me since childhood.

It may sound simplistic, but it is about right and wrong. When I believe a course of action is required then my heart tells me to get on with it and believe in it because my actions are executed for the right reasons. Here is a case study to illustrate what I mean.

Police officers in the United Kingdom are represented by a Federation. In 1919, there was a police strike. The ringleaders of the police union were arrested and jailed. The Police Federation was formed by the government as the sole recognised representative body for police in the United Kingdom. This is unique in terms of law enforcement agencies in the western world who are represented by unions. The result is that officers lack the employment rights that others enjoy. This includes their Terms and Conditions. There is no right to withdraw their labour. The implications are that the wellbeing and human rights of police officers are highly vulnerable to being undermined.

In a famous case in the Netherlands whilst engaged in a dispute with the Government, the Dutch Police Union threatened to withdraw officers from performing public order duties on overtime at major football games. The dispute was settled within twenty-four hours.

The culture of the Federation could at best be described as 'not rocking the boat'. The senior Federation officials of each police force are paid as chief inspectors, which is pensionable. Many of the officials are of more junior rank. They have a vested interest in the status quo.

In 2010, the Conservative-led coalition at the behest of the then Prime Minister determined to 'reform' the police service in the United Kingdom. The action taken was to cut police budgets by 20%. This resulted in the loss of 15% of the active-duty officers – a staggering loss of almost 23,000 personnel. Since staffing costs were on average 80% of budgets, police departments resorted to desperate measures to make up the difference. These included brigading of forces to provide joint services across several police forces. The message put out to the public message was these cuts were efficiency gains. But make no mistake about it, this was all about cost-cutting, pure and simple. Another strategy to make up the shortfall was to sell capital assets, in the form of police stations, which were used as revenue streams.

The most significant impact of this decimation was the erosion, in a meaningful sense, of non-confrontational contact between the police and the public. Police officers who had built up connectivity with local partner agencies were given wider geographical areas of responsibility. Increasingly, Police Community Support Officers (PCSO) were substituted for officers. The perceived wisdom by government and executive-level police' leaders' was that officers who could complete the full range of operations, including arrests, were now a luxury that could not be afforded to deliver reassurance by consistency of relationships with the public, and partner agencies.

PCSOs wore a similar uniform to police officers. They had no personal protective equipment (PPE) and no power of arrest. If necessary, they told an offender to remain on-site for thirty minutes until a police officer arrived!

PCSOs were regarded by Executive-level police leaders, as a cheaper option to police officers. This economic argument was transformed by the government cutting the starting pay of police officers by £4k. This had the effect that a PCSO cost more money than an officer of up to four years' service.

The net effect was to destroy, in a meaningful sense, policing for the public as originally envisaged by Sir Robert Peel in 1829 when he founded the Metropolitan Police in London. (see Appendix 1.)

The Police Federation cited the cost and futility of challenging the status quo and seeking the same employment rights as enjoyed by our western counterparts. The Federation had a legal firm on retainer. They had at that time, over £85 million in strategic reserve. The Federation kept referring to 'Industrial Rights' to besmirch the cause.

I was a serving police inspector at that time. I researched the subject and decided that the failure of the Federation to protect the terms and conditions of its members was a Breach of Article 11 of the Human Rights Act, which protects the right to freedom of assembly and association. In my personal time, I contacted legal companies who were prominent in successfully challenging the Government on Human Rights cases. The Solicitors and Barristers agreed with my contention that it was in the wider interests of the public and police for officers to have the right to form a union. I founded an organisation with a colleague called Police Choice. Its purpose was to obtain full employment rights for police officers in the UK. Our Legal Team drafted a 'Letter before Action'. This was the document that would be sent to the Home Secretary, the member of the government with direct responsibility for Policing and Criminal Justice.

Only 200 signatures from serving officers were required to initiate proceedings. Their signature would confirm that they believed themselves to be disadvantaged by being denied the opportunity to join a Union. We were aware that officers were fearful of repercussions.

Throughout, I had never hidden my name and identity as a police officer. However, the lawyers drafted confirmation of the protection in law for the proposed action.

It read:

following legal advice from leading Human Rights Law Firm, Leigh Day & Co and Barristers from Matrix Chambers, who confirmed that Police Officers who:

1. *Donate to a fighting fund the purpose of which is to fund legal action designed to secure for police officers the right to join a union; and/or*
2. *Join as applicants in such a legal action; and/or*
3. *Become members of a support network relating to that action These actions, of themselves, will be entirely lawful and not breach the strict Police Act which bars policemen and policewomen from belonging to or affiliating with a trade union.*

Unfortunately, police officers were fearful of repercussions and played safe. The required 200 signatures took over two years to gather. This fatally undermined the credibility of the case according to the legal team.

Throughout the years of promoting this challenge, both as a serving and then a retired officer, I believed in the correctness of my actions and always identified myself by name and rank. I was able to look at myself in the mirror, I could believe in the rightness of my actions, and sought to provide colleagues and former colleagues, the benefits of union membership as befits a police organisation in the 21st century. The feedback that I received was that police officers accepted my rationale for change but were fearful of ruining their police careers. Too bad they did not understand the importance of the words of Theodore Roosevelt.

THE MAN IN THE ARENA

"IT IS NOT THE CRITIC WHO COUNTS; NOT THE MAN WHO POINTS OUT HOW THE STRONG MAN STUMBLES, OR WHERE THE DOER OF DEEDS COULD HAVE DONE THEM BETTER. THE CREDIT BELONGS TO THE MAN WHO IS ACTUALLY IN THE ARENA, WHOSE FACE IS MARRED BY DUST AND SWEAT AND BLOOD; WHO STRIVES VALIANTLY; WHO ERRS, WHO COMES SHORT AGAIN AND AGAIN, BECAUSE THERE IS NO EFFORT WITHOUT ERROR AND SHORTCOMING; BUT WHO DOES ACTUALLY STRIVE TO DO THE DEEDS; WHO KNOWS GREAT ENTHUSIASMS, THE GREAT DEVOTIONS; WHO SPENDS HIMSELF IN A WORTHY CAUSE; WHO AT THE BEST KNOWS IN THE END THE TRIUMPH OF HIGH ACHIEVEMENT, AND WHO AT THE WORST, IF HE FAILS, AT LEAST FAILS WHILE DARING GREATLY. SO THAT HIS PLACE SHALL NEVER BE WITH THOSE COLD AND TIMID SOULS WHO NEITHER KNOW VICTORY NOR DEFEAT."

Theodore Roosevelt

LEARN & LEAD

A journey of discovery that never ends

"A leader is like a shepherd.
"He stays behind the flock, letting the most nimble go out ahead, "Whereupon the others follow,
"Not realising, that all along, they are being directed from behind."

Nelson MANDELA

Chapter Eleven

Developing Yourself as a Leader

The skillset we possess as a Leader is the product of several actions we take. At its best, the leaders will help and encourage the team members to grow in such a manner that they will become the leaders of the future.

At its worst are those people who have closed minds. Their leadership philosophy can be summed up as 'my way or the highway'.

One of the most liberating aspects of Leadership for me was the realisation that leadership is not about being the best at everything – understanding that the true measure of success as a leader is not personal recognition. Leadership should be focused on the morale and effectiveness of those for whom we are responsible.

As a leader, I am responsible for the outcomes of my teams. That is not to say that individuality must be squashed at every turn. It is the leader's responsibility to create the Values, environment and culture of their organisation so that our team members thrive with appropriate trust and responsibility thus being able to deliver their best quality of performance.

This is not reckless laissez-faire but authentic trust between the leader and the team. It is based on knowing ourselves and our team as people and behaving accordingly. Trust is the cement that binds the team together.

The prerequisite is that we objectively assess the calibre and capability of our reports at the earliest opportunity. Ideally, this evaluation is based upon our direct knowledge. Sometimes, however, the size of our organisation may preclude this desirable methodology. When this is the case, the assessment of trusted subordinates and colleagues, with line responsibility is a good foundation pending our own findings.

Overconfidence in a leader as to their own or other's abilities is damaging on many levels for the team. Confidence, born of relevant operational experience and combined with an open, inquiring mind, is my preferred state.

Similarly, diffidence or inability to make rational decisions (which may include putting our reports in harm's way) is equally disastrous for the wellbeing of ourselves and others.

Good Leadership is founded upon knowing our own limitations, understanding their impact on decision-making, and accepting appropriate support to enhance the quality of actions.

Continuous Professional Development (CPD) is not restricted to technical or professional knowledge. It embraces a desire to improve our Emotional Intelligence, that is, how we improve our communication and understanding of people.

I was fortunate to learn about Kaizen, the Japanese philosophy of continuous improvement. I was a senior police leader at the time and the training was provided by the Honda Motor Company as part of their Social Responsibility Programme. This resonated with my belief that it is everyone's responsibility to move an organisation forward, not just the person in a designated position of responsibility.

In future roles, I adapted the Kaizen Quality Circle methodology for my police responsibilities. Once I had accurately and objectively ascertained the people in my teams, I began to pose questions. These inquiries were separated by a few months at a time.

- The first question was "What are the systems and processes that prevent you from delivering your best performance and how can we improve them?"
- The second question was "What are your ideas for improving the quality of the performance of our team and how could we implement them?"
- The third question was "If you led this team, what would be your priorities to improve our quality of performance and why have you chosen them?"

With each question, the originator was given the responsibility to pilot their idea. If it proved successful, it was rolled out across the borough. If it proved unsuccessful in that format, the originator could amend and adjust their ideas in the light of experience. There was no such thing as a bad idea.

My first posting as an Inspector was to inherit responsibility for a demoralised team.

In operational performance terms, the team had traditionally languished in the last place out of five teams. After six months, we were in the third position. At the end of that year, we were top performers and for the remaining three years I was based with that team.

It is important to note, that at no stage did I ever refer to the numerically- based 'targets' set for the five 'response 'teams.

Rather, by facilitating the development and critical thinking of the team, they consistently delivered their best quality of performance. In effect, 'the numbers looked after themselves'.

My focus was on developing myself so that I could be the best leader I could be to transform a downbeat, defeatist culture to an invigorated confident team. They knew that I 'had their back' because we knew and trusted one another.

In the police force, I was fortunate to benefit from studying an Executive Diploma in Leadership and Management that was delivered by an external consultancy. There were some twenty fellow Inspectors in my cohort.

One of the modules made a particularly indelible impression on me. The title of the module was 'Coaching as a Leadership Style'. This was a significant divergence from the traditional and widespread 'Command and Control' style that was prevalent in the police at the time. The norm was for people to be ordered by more senior colleagues to perform their duty in a specified way based on their respective ranks.

The facilitator decided to illustrate the skill through a role play. I was chosen to be an Inspector who had to use a coaching style to deal with a colleague who was a poor performer but was reluctant to admit that fact. My fellow actor was deliberately chosen for his role as he was a high performer and hated poor performance. My colleague and I were situated in the middle of the large room. The remaining colleagues sat around the edges of the room. My attention was focused entirely on my colleague.

Using Emotional Intelligence and Neuro-Linguistic Programming (NLP) techniques, such as body language and tone of voice that I had learned as a detective, the room faded from my thinking. It was challenging using this new style of Leadership in such a tough situation, but it began to become easier.

I used Active Listening to evaluate what was being said by my colleague, how he said it, and what was not being said rather than having a predetermined agenda to enforce my questions on him regardless of his answers.

The scenario felt real for both of us.

The feedback from my colleague, was that, in effect, his answers, were leaving him with increasingly less room to manoeuvre for his next answer was based entirely on his responses to me. I saw a palpable change come over my colleague in terms of his demeanour, body language, and vocal style. In essence, he became that person for real. The scenario concluded with my colleague admitting that he was a poor performer and reluctant to admit it.

In the end, the facilitator said, "I can see you're well practised at interrogations and interviews. I'd chosen you because I was aware of your detective background."

I replied, "This was an interview in which by actively listening, the other person reduced his opportunities to deny his true position by his own words."

Afterward, I asked my colleague how the roleplay had been for him. He said, "It became real. By listening to what I was saying and how it was being said, I felt like I was in a funnel that was increasingly narrowing. It left me no opportunity to escape."

There were two major lessons that I learned from the Executive Diploma in Leadership and Management. Firstly, the critical significance of knowing myself and continuing to learn more about the qualities of leadership that would help me grow in my leadership responsibilities.

Secondly, helping those for whom I was responsible to grow in the same manner by teaching what I learned and giving them the same opportunities to go to professional training as they demonstrated their growth potential.

"Knowing others is intelligence. "Knowing yourself is true wisdom. "Mastering others is strength. "Mastering yourself is true power."

Lao TZU

Celebrate success without hubris or complacency

"A strong leader finds strength in others and builds them up, "A poor leader picks at weaknesses and breaks others down."

Andrea MARSHALL

Chapter Twelve

Leadership Means Knowing Your People

Our use of language, tonality, body language, and an accurate background intelligence (e.g., families, birthdays, interests, etc.) of the people we manage, and lead is critically important.

Police organisations are disciplined bodies with a plethora of rules and regulations that govern behaviours. Also, they must adhere to the sanctions of the law.

When I was a senior leader in the police, I never referred to people as 'my command' but as 'those for whom I am responsible.'

The strategic decision-making body for each operational policing unit had been known for many years as 'The Senior Leadership Team'. (SLT) It was indicative of a different mindset by executive-level colleagues, when the organisation was reshaped to be based on groups of boroughs called 'Areas' to change the term 'Senior Leadership Team' to 'Area Command Team' (ACT). This change was cascaded and adopted by Areas and Departments. The prevalent poor communication style was exacerbated by the invariable use of emails as a more 'efficient and effective' method of speaking with the 'grunts,' as operational people were so regarded. This Faux Leadership demonstrated absolutely no interest in developing mutual trust, confidence, and respect with other staff at successive levels. They certainly would not see it as part of their role profile to know staff outside their circle as people. Pretending you are demonstrating outstanding leadership traits under this operating scenario does not make it so.

I learned the truism of a phrase of mine on my second day of being an Acting Sergeant. The phrase is – Leadership is knowing ourselves and those for whom we have responsibility as people and behaving accordingly.

The date was Thursday, April 14, 1988. A friend and colleague, Frank Mason, was murdered off duty that morning a few hours before starting work on the team I had just joined as an Acting Sergeant. At such a raw time for everyone in the organisation, the emotions bubbled over amongst those he had been working alongside.

It was traditional for many team briefings in my police department to be accompanied by a cup of tea.

The Management Team, as it was called then, consisted of our Inspector, another Sergeant, and me. I carried the tray complete with teapot, cups, milk, sugar, and biscuits. Truth be told, it was like a prop for me.

Everyone on the team was openly crying. I knew many of the people in that room but had never worked with them before. After a decent interval, the Inspector advised us all that our patrol and operational responsibilities that day would be undertaken by other colleagues. That was the correct decision. The implications of traumatised officers engaging across the range of interactions with the public did not bear thinking about. The members of the team began to compose themselves. They could begin to see that we regarded them as people with emotional requirements – not caricatures of Robocop.

The room was quiet. Tentatively, I scanned the faces of my colleagues. They were traumatised and started asking questions about the circumstances of the murder. This was a key moment. Despite their feelings, they were beginning to think like police officers again. We undertook to find out as much detail as possible to update them appropriately during the day.

I then judged the moment right to pass the biscuits around the table and take requests for tea preferences. We then offered the team a choice. Remain in the police station or to park their police car at a location chosen by themselves to be conducive for reflection and contemplation of the day's events. Before the team dispersed, the Inspector informed everyone on the team to attend the nearby police sports and social club at the end of the shift. This permitted the start of the diffusion process for individuals and the re-establishing of the team ethic.

The sun was shining, the sky was blue. The weather seemed incongruous for the enormity of the day's events. I chose to park my patrol car in a specific location that I knew to be peaceful. Whenever I pass by that location, my mind is transported back to that day. The memory never loses its intensity.

The day illustrated the critical importance of an emotionally intelligent knowledge of those for whom we are responsible. Twenty years later, I became responsible for the coordination and planning of the commemorative event. Knowing the unpredictability of British weather, I arranged for a gazebo with retractable side covers to be hired. Other planning colleagues ridiculed my decision as the cost was significant. My views were that I did not intend to make the success of the day weather dependent. My role involved contacting everyone associated with the original incident. I learned of their perspective of the day. In many cases, it reignited the trauma of that day for them and myself.

One of the most powerful and moving aspects of the anniversary event occurred when Frank's mum was speaking about him. The sky was blue and sunny like all those years before. She had just said how much she missed Frank every day when the sky went black and there was a crack of thunder that sounded like a bomb explosion. Then the torrential rain fell. Everyone was grateful for the gazebo.

Another situation concerned my friend and fellow Acting Inspector George. We were both taking part in the same process – to be promoted as substantive Inspectors. We supported each other in role-playing our evidence for the impending interview part of the process. This was the decisive stage that determined success or failure.

I passed and George failed. He was devastated. My feeling of success was tainted. George was a stalwart for me in good times and bad. I knew that George's evidence, properly presented, should have enabled him to pass the Promotion Board. I knew that he was a confident person who deserved promotion. I could not understand why and how he had failed this process. George was articulate, knew the venue, and the members of the Board and their vagaries. It was inexplicable.

I asked him to describe what had happened. He told me that throughout his interview he had struggled to hear the questions put to him and to make himself heard. I asked why this was the case. He told me that the police helicopter was practising landing and lifting off from the field outside the interview room. I checked and no other candidate had had to compete with the sound of a helicopter ascending and descending for one hour outside the window of the interview room. I asked him if he was going to appeal the decision. He said there was no point as the organisation would not admit that due process had not been followed and no appeal had ever succeeded. I asked his permission to appeal on his behalf. He agreed.

I researched the terms and conditions of the process and there was an appeal section. The only grounds acceptable were discrimination against a candidate. I sought and obtained a meeting with the senior officer who had management responsibility for the promotion process.

He trivialised the impact of the helicopter's actions. I argued that the process was of itself stressful – the noise level was challenging for George to gather his thoughts and present his evidence. It was also challenging for the interview panel to accurately hear the evidence, evaluate it, and record it. I asked how many other candidates had endured the helicopter impact. No one else had experienced this significant interruption.

I suggested that a fresh panel be convened to permit George to give his evidence appropriately or that the appeal be allowed. Otherwise, George had been discriminated against. I was informed to put my appeal in writing which would be subject to the final decision of the Deputy Chief Constable. I did so.

A week later, I was finishing night duty at a police station. I met George, who was smiling and holding a piece of paper. "The appeal has been allowed. Thank you." I felt blessed to have been able to repay the support George had given to me over the years.

Another aspect of Leadership concerns how to respond to poor performers. When I inherited responsibility for a unit, department, or team, my first action was to research their behaviours and performance. I was interested in receiving a handover from my predecessor. I would not be bound by their feedback, but it was a useful starting point. It also would tell me about the standards of my predecessor. I would evaluate the performance indicators but was more interested in the quality of their performance and their outcomes.

I would then first hold 121 meetings with my inherited perceived poor performers. It was essential to quickly ascertain is this a case of 'can't do' or 'won't do'? The former received appropriate support and opportunities for development from me to raise their level to that required. The latter faced starker choices. I explained that my motivation was to ensure fairness for all those I led. Their deliberate underperformance undermined morale and team cohesion. This was unfair to the rest of us. Their choice consisted of shape up or ship out.

The more positive aspects of Leadership cannot be developed until you have a coherent team whose values reflect that of yourself on behalf of the organisation.

When I had operational responsibility for Contingency Planning and Resource Management for two boroughs, I worked alternate weekends.

I noticed that every Sunday that I was working, that one of the sergeants on my team continued to be in his office when his tour of duty was finished.

He was known to be meticulous.

The sergeant was middle aged, married with two daughters.

I always checked in on him during the shift, and at the end of the tour of duty.

He would tell me that he was just finishing a piece of work. I checked his duty records.

He was not claiming overtime.

One Saturday, I was not rostered to work, and neither was the sergeant.

I needed to collect some documents for a significant meeting on the following Monday.

The sergeant's office was in the same corridor as mine.

I noticed that the door was closed, but there was a light on.

I opened the door, and found the sergeant sitting at his desk, listening to a commercial radio station. He was in civilian clothes.

I asked him why he was there.

He said his wife was shopping for clothes in a nearby department store, and he preferred to wait there.

I noticed that he never finished his duty on time but was not claiming overtime.

I was becoming extremely concerned.

I then spoke to another member of the team privately.

I explained that I was concerned that the sergeant was spending a lot of unauthorised time in his office and there did not appear to be an operational reason for that.

The officer told me in confidence that the sergeant had found out his wife had a lover within the police and could not face going home to the family unit.

I thanked the officer and respected his confidence.

I then adjusted my weekend working so that I could check on the sergeant on a day he was not rostered to work.

I saw that he was in the office so made us both a cup of tea and closed the door in his office behind me.

I said, "What's going on? I'm concerned about you."
He suddenly burst into tears and held his head in his hands.
He said his wife was leaving him for another man.
I asked why he hadn't sought my help.

He said he felt useless, a failure and was worried that his colleagues would see him as a figure of fun.

I said, knowing your work colleagues as I do, the last thing they will do is make fun of you at such a terrible time.

The break-up of a marriage is traumatic for everyone and a genuine tragedy.

I offered help and support in whatever way worked for him.

The only condition was that he did not hibernate in his office.

We worked on his professional development and enabled him to take sufficient personal time as the circumstances demanded. He only needed to advise me of his needs, and I would ensure he was supported.

In due course, the sergeant recovered from the trauma of his divorce.

To this day, only he and I know the details of his situation, and how we managed it, confidentially.

Those for whom we are responsible, are not robots, but sentient human beings.

Understanding our people as the individuals they are is the most significant aspect of Leadership.

We need to be able to trust each other to perform in all circumstances; and reach out for pastoral support when required.

People are truly the greatest asset of an organisation if we treat each other appropriately and fairly.

"Emotional Intelligence is not about being nice.
"It's about managing your emotions to achieve the best possible outcomes."

Travis BRADBERRY

APPENDIX ONE

Home Office
FOI release
Definition of policing by consent
Published 10 December 2012

When saying 'policing by consent', the Home Secretary was referring to a long-standing philosophy of British policing, known as the Robert Peel's nine Principles of Policing. However, there is no evidence of any link to Robert Peel and it was likely devised by the first Commissioners of Police of the Metropolis (Charles Rowan and Richard Mayne). The principles which were set out in the 'General Instructions' that were issued to every new police officer from 1829 were:

1. To prevent crime and disorder, as an alternative to their repression by military force and severity of legal punishment.
2. To recognise always that the power of the police to fulfil their functions and duties is dependent on public approval of their existence, actions, and behaviour and on their ability to secure and maintain public respect.
3. To recognise always that to secure and maintain the respect and approval of the public means also the securing of the willing co-operation of the public in the task of securing observance of laws.
4. To recognise always that the extent to which the co-operation of the public can be secured diminishes proportionately the necessity of the use of physical force and compulsion for achieving police objectives.
5. To seek and preserve public favour, not by pandering to public opinion; but by constantly demonstrating absolutely impartial service to law, in complete independence of policy, and without regard to the justice or injustice of the substance of individual laws, by ready offering of individual service and friendship to all members of the public without regard to their wealth or

social standing, by ready exercise of courtesy and friendly good humour; and by ready offering of individual sacrifice in protecting and preserving life.

6. To use physical force only when the exercise of persuasion, advice and warning is found to be insufficient to obtain public co- operation to an extent necessary to secure observance of law or to restore order, and to use only the minimum degree of physical force which is necessary on any particular occasion for achieving a police objective.

7. To maintain at all times a relationship with the public that gives reality to the historic tradition that the police are the public and that the public are the police, the police being only members of the public who are paid to give full time attention to duties which are incumbent on every citizen in the interests of community welfare and existence.

8. To recognise always the need for strict adherence to police-executive functions, and to refrain from even seeming to usurp the powers of the judiciary of avenging individuals or the State, and of authoritatively judging guilt and punishing the guilty.

9. To recognise always that the test of police efficiency is the absence of crime and disorder, and not the visible evidence of police action in dealing with them.

Essentially, as explained by the notable police historian Charles Reith in his *New Study of Police History* in 1956, it was a philosophy of policing 'unique in history and throughout the world because it derived not from fear but almost exclusively from public co-operation with the police, induced by them designedly by behaviour which secures and maintains for them the approval, respect and affection of the public'.

It should be noted that it refers to the power of the police coming from the common consent of the public, as opposed to the power of the state. It does not mean the consent of an individual. No individual can choose to withdraw his or her consent from the police, or from a law.

APPENDIX TWO

Countries that do not routinely arm their police.

- Botswana
- Cook Islands
- Fiji
- Iceland
- Ireland
- Kiribati
- Malawi
- Marshall Islands
- Nauru
- New Zealand
- Niue
- Norway
- Samoa
- Solomon Islands
- Tonga
- Tuvalu
- United Kingdom
- Vanuatu
- Virgin Islands (US)

Epilogue: my perspective on 'The ESSENTIAL Heart of a Leader

Managers deserve and require support and training to know how to be able to manage people effectively and fairly.

Leadership is not a rank, role, or job title, it is a mindset.

- Leadership is a service function.
- Leadership is knowing ourselves and those we are responsible for as people and behaving accordingly.
- The role is not the person.
- Leadership should not be endured but enjoyed.
- Leadership is not about being the best at everything.
- Leadership is not knowing everything.
- The people performing their roles invariably know how to do their best.
- Leadership means taking effective ACTION against the wilfully poor, toxic performers as a prerequisite to your future credibility.
- Such wilfully poor, toxic performers (not the inexperienced) are akin to delinquents. They KNOW what they are doing.
- Others also know this and are waiting to see what you do and how you resolve this contradiction in the culture you espouse.
- Leadership is to say to your reports "What do you need "?
- **Leaders are people too.**
- Leaders have private lives which are as important to them as they are to you.
- Leaders retain ultimate responsibility for their team, department, or organisation.